VICTORIO[
A LADIES' MAN

A Biography of King Charles VII of France (1403–1461)

By
Caroline (Cally) Rogers Neill Sehnaoui

Strategic Book Publishing and Rights Co.

Strategic Book Publishing and Rights Co.
12620 FM 1960, Suite A4-507
Houston, TX 77065
www.sbpra.com

ISBN 978-1-62516-049-2

Typography and page composition by J. K. Eckert & Company

To my beloved husband, Elie,

and my lovely children, Anthony, Caroline, and Alexander,

who encouraged me and accompanied me with love.

Contents

PREAMBLE
(AUTHOR'S PRELUDE)

Cleopatra, born to the last king of the 300-year-old Macedonian dynasty in 69 BC, had not a drop of Egyptian blood and was the last ruler of the Ptolemaic era. Though not a beauty, as is commonly thought, she had great energy, depth of intelligence, and pure cunning. Plutarch wrote of her that "her voice was like an instrument of many strings" and that she had at her command "a thousand forms of flattery."

Having seduced Julius Caesar in 47 BC, during his attempt to conquer Egypt, Cleopatra then bore him a son and moved to a lavish villa outside Rome. There she lived, unpopular and distant, until Caesar's murder in 44 BC. Cicero wrote that the Romans held her in low regard.

Returning to Egypt with her young son, Caesarion, she watched and waited for her second campaign to power. This opportunity appeared in the form of Mark Antony, the heir-general to Caesar. When she met Mark Antony in Tarsus (in today's Turkey) she so overwhelmed him with gifts and charm that he put off his plans to conquer Persia and returned with her to Alexandria in her trademark gilded barge, red sails to the wind.

There they lived a life of folly and debauchery, paraded before the people seated on golden thrones. She and Mark Antony had three children. Eleven years after they left for Alexandria, Cleopatra realized that Mark Antony was a dissipated and ruined man. She sought then to form an alliance with the Emperor Octavian and tricked Mark Antony into suicide. She was 39 and had been queen for 22 years. When her attempt to captivate the young emperor failed, she had no choice but to take her own life. She was buried in Alexandria next to her beloved Mark Antony.

Having won over the two greatest Romans of her day her failure to befriend Octavian cost her, her own life. She was greedy for power, and Egypt too was lost. But her name, two thousand years later, still suggests lust, life, power, intelligence, and extravagance.

I chose Cleopatra as the image of powerful women who represent the personal branding par excellence of women of the centuries before our time. Of course there are many others; we must remember the awesome qualities of these female powerhouses who were exceptional for their own time, who overcame a world dominated by men, and who were "brands" in their own right.

Although it is impossible in this short book to credit the many women who are unforgettable, personally endowed with qualities and situations entirely unique to them, I will cite a few who are known to even those who are not history buffs. To begin, courageous Saint Joan of Arc, the cool and clever, and virgin Queen Elizabeth I of England and her hot-headed cousin Mary, Queen of Scots. Who can forget Pocahontas, the strong-minded daughter of Powhatan, who prevented large-scale battles between the American colonists and the native southern Indian tribes? All for the love of an Englishman. Let us glide through time to meet Boadicea, Eleanor of Aquitaine (twice queen, of France and England, and the most powerful woman of her era), Margaret Thatcher, the Iron Lady, and perhaps, soon, Hillary Clinton. These women have one thing in common: their determined quest for power.

There have always been power-seekers. Plato wrote in *The Republic* that everyone had his goal (or price): power, fame, or fortune. Still under the subject of power come the great conquerors: Alexander the Great, Julius Caesar, and Hannibal and his army crossing the Alps on elephant back. The three of them they wielded total power over three continents for many centuries. Later came Attila the Hun, Charlemagne, the Vikings, the Normans, and Napoleon Bonaparte; each leader led his conquests from north to south and east to west, and their armies influenced the world in many ways. Think, for example, of William the Conqueror: He changed the habits, language, food, dress, and even the laws of the British Isles.

In his incomparable analysis Plato does seem to omit passion, dedication, and compassion. Many dozens of men and women who hold a place in our hearts and minds were personal brands, or standards, in a way for their search to improve mankind and will always appear in capital points of history. I think of Marie Curie, Louis Pasteur, Florence Nightingale, Eleanor Roosevelt, Albert Einstein, Jonas Salk, Ian Fleming (the doctor), and many others who were not working for glory but for the good of the people and the betterment of the future in science, health, and sociology. Theirs were not paths to power or riches, but a way to improve the plight of mankind.

During the sixteenth century, Europe produced two royal giants of cultural, on one hand, and religious, on the other, revolutions: Louis the XIV and Henry VIII. Louis XIV was the Sun King, and his stamp (or brand) was on every one of his many endeavors to make France the pinnacle of culture, elegance, and evolution on all levels. He marked palaces and architecture, to etiquette and fashion, furniture and food, literature, music, art, and the most famous lifestyle in history. Versailles and the stylized sun (a sort of logo) became the symbol of grandeur for all time. Even his most famous mistresses, Madame de Montespan and Madame de Maintenon, entered French history on their own individuality. The first was a beautiful and extremely able mistress whose family, she considered, was far nobler than the king's own line! The second was calculating while seemingly unassuming and made him comfortable in many simple ways, especially just being seen in her presence; it is largely agreed that he secretly married Madame de Maintenon in old age.

The death of Louis XIII when Louis was not quite five left the young king guideless, raised by servants and neglected by his mother. When he was nine the nobles and the Paris Parliament rose against Cardinal Mazarin and the Crown; this marked the outset of the Fronde. Louis suffered humiliation and fear during these years, which would mark him forever. For the rest of his long life Louis XIV mistrusted Paris, the nobles, and the common people.

The Fronde over, Louis became an apt pupil of Mazarin, who taught him the arts, the intricacies of administration, and love of display. Upon the death of Mazarin, the young king, aged 23, declared he could handle the reins of government alone. This was to be a dictatorship by divine right, a first in French history.

Plato's life choices were clearly answered by the Sun King in his own *Mémoires*. He wrote, "In my heart I prefer fame above all else, even life itself."

Fame was certainly to be his. Louis XIV worked eight hours a day, personally supervising the enormous tasks that lay before him. Versailles became the epitome of splendor, and with the sun as his emblem, Louis was so renowned around the world as to almost be mythical. Louis built up the navy, ports, roads, canals, and police force. Molière and Racine sang his praises, and the landscape of France changed under his rule. The Académie Française, the Invalides, and hundreds of other buildings and monuments were erected under his orders. By the time he reached middle age, the Sun King was at his zenith.

Before the end of the seventeenth century, however, his decline had begun. He irritated his neighbors (Germany, Spain, and England), lost some of his wars, and revoked the Edict of Nantes. When he died in 1715 at the age of 77, he had weakened the nobility and lived in glorious isolation. No one in history, however, has associated the Sun King with anything but magnificence—it was his personal brand. Voltaire wrote of him, "His name can never be pronounced without respect and without summoning the image of an eternally memorable age."

During the late 18th and early 19th centuries one man stands out above all others: Napoleon Bonaparte. General and great military tactician, Consul, and Emperor, Napoleon changed the map of Europe, created a new system of laws, and will forever be remembered for his stance—hand inside his jacket. His years of greatness exhilarating, his years of exile humiliating, he is a brand he created through his genius.

Another name for the nineteenth century is the Victorian Era. Queen Victoria was short, stout, and retiring and wore "widows" weeds most of her reign. Her personal brand was dull, prudish, and strict, yet she placed most of her children on thrones all over Europe and became Empress of the British Empire, the superpower of the century.

Abraham Lincoln's brand was his tall, thin stature; sad face; top hat; and all-black ensembles. He reunited a growing nation; pushed the frontiers westward; and most important, abolished slavery, changing the economic demographics of a nation.

Winston Churchill was an orator, statesman, and author. He is thus branded for all time. He was born in 1874 to a descendant of the Dukes of Marlborough and an American beauty. His life was devoted in peacetime and during times of war to unity and friendship between the two peoples of his dual ancestry. Encouraged to make his career in the army, he soon tired of military life and decided to earn his living in writing and politics. Covering the war in South Africa for a London newspaper was the onset of his popularity. Escaping from a Boer prison he returned to England a hero and won a seat in the House of Commons in 1900.

An imposing, large man with a bulldog face and bright-red hair, Churchill had a turbulent political career, changing his constituencies, securing various ministerial posts in the cabinet, even switching party affiliation in the minute it took him to cross from the Conservative benches in Parliament to join the Liberal party across the floor. At the outbreak of World War I the British navy was in a state of readiness thanks to Churchill, long suspicious of the Germans. Not only did he enlarge the navy, but also he oversaw the development and rapid production of the tank, which greatly helped the allies on the western front. Though he thrived during wartime, Churchill would spend the twenty years between the Great Wars in and out of government, powerful then powerless. During these years he wrote two books that sold very well: *The World Crisis* and *Marlborough: His Life and Times.* The sales of the first book, in 1923, allowed him to buy Chartwell, the manor house in Kent that would be home to him for the rest of his long life.

After the removal of his appendix, Churchill declared himself to be "without an office, without a seat, without a party, and even without an appendix."

The early days of World War II found Churchill at the height of his importance to the nation. It seemed that crises brought out his patriotism, inexhaustible energy, and ability to concentrate and made him one of the greatest speakers of all time. Britain declared war on Germany in the fall of 1939; by the following spring Winston Churchill was Prime Minister of Great Britain. Wartime legislature would give him emergency powers greater than any Prime Minister in modern English history. In this situation Churchill will be remembered forever, giving his famous V sign, smoking his cigar, visiting damaged parts of the country, and speaking nationally on the radio. He became hugely popular, joining the people in Britain's "finest hour."

After the Allied victory in which he played such a central part, Churchill participated as opposition leader in all the great post-war conferences where he warned of a Russian takeover of Eastern European countries left hanging in the political void of the German defeat. Foreign policy became his major battle-horse. He invented the term "iron curtain" to describe the Communist-Soviet menace and sought approval of a European Union. During these years he published the six volumes of *The Second World War,* a masterful opus, himself one of the architects of that war.

After six years on the fringe, Churchill once again became Prime Minister toward the end of 1951. Suffering intermittently from ill health, he retired in 1955, having won the Order of the Garter (with the right to be called Sir Winston) and the Nobel Prize for Literature. While serving another ten years in the House of Commons he also produced yet another major work, the four-volume *A History of the English-Speaking Peoples.*

Of Plato's choices for mankind I have so far omitted fortune, because power, fame, and fortune are inter-related. Many famous people had power, and some had fortune, too, but I am addressing the predominant personal brand. As far as riches are concerned we must turn back to the times of Midas and Croesus to King Herod and the incredibly rich seventeenth century Dutchman Jan Sic, who was the patron of Rembrandt and paid today's equivalent of $32,000 for a single tulip bulb! These men were principally known for their fortunes as are Bill Gates, Warren Buffett, Steve Jobs, and Donald Trump today. Fortune often brings fame, and fame can bring fortune, although a power-seeker may not want anything but power.

These people were branded for improving standards of living and creating brands for their countries' military, industrial, and educational progress. It should not be forgotten that people the world over owe so much to these emblems of greatness.

The twentieth century has brought a new element to the realm of personal branding: first quicker; wider; and, for years now, immediate communication. At the beginning it was newspapers and the telephone, then films, recordings, radio, television, and the computer. People take instant communication for granted today; the world has become smaller and it is much easier to become famous, make a fortune, or wield power. We all have some knowledge of many infamous cases, from Al Capone to Timothy McVeigh, OJ Simpson to the bitter and perverse Osama bin Laden. We have seen them on the screen; we have heard them speak; we feel we know them.

On the pleasant side we also are familiar with Charlie Chaplin, Clark Gable, Marilyn Monroe, and Ernest Hemingway. Thanks to inexpensive books, films and recordings, and TV and radio, we have personal contact with the personal brands of writers, actors, singers, and even composers from centuries past. Also, doctors, economists, engineers and architects, queens, and religious leaders are better known by the world's population.

Thanks to the media we are up on current events, and we can join together to detest Mugabe and admire Nelson Mandela. Thanks to the media we still buy or watch anything and everything about the late Diana of Wales. And thanks to the media a girl with little to offer has risen to fame—I have Paris Hilton in mind. The media are the power of today, and famous is the by-word. In the fifties Gary Cooper and James Stewart, Eisenhower and de Gaulle didn't have a fraction of the fame that Nicolas Sarkozy or Brad Pitt enjoy today. It will be difficult for historians of the future to sort out the worthy from the riffraff. The first part of the past century produced many great statesmen; the past sixty years have given us some unforgettable politicians. This century has us on a media-controlled celebrity chase. Junky tabloids fly off the shelves, whereas serious newspapers have a relatively low readership.

Fashion models until the 1960s, were nameless, barring a very few; today they are icons. Any waiter at Maxim's can tell you that the best tables are given to people whose PR agents have booked for them because they are famous in some circles. This is probably not lasting fame, like that of Onassis or the Windsors who were well-known at Maxim's for 30 years, a longer time than, say, Prince Alwaleed bin Talal. Not that Maxim's is the ultimate address, but simply a good restaurant known for being the place where the elite meet. In any case, most people who seek popularity through the press, when famous, clamor for privacy. Greta Garbo ("I want to be alone") is a case in point, as are dozens of others today.

While Howard Hughes and Charles Lindbergh will go down in aviation history, so will Richard Branson, although with fewer lines in the encyclopedias. Let us see which among my selected modern, public-relations-dependent subjects are lasting personalities and which are, in slang, those who are just a flash-in-the-pan. My admiration tends to the amazing Martha Stewart and the twenty-first century superman, Branson.

PROLOGUE

Our book on King Charles VII of France goes back centuries, offering thorough research on the comparatively little known man or king. We do know that he was a contemporary of Joan of Arc, played a major role in bringing his country out of the abyss, and helped develop it after going through wars at home and against the English through developments of the arts and many infrastructure undertakings of a magnitude little known before his reign. It will also introduce us to a very beautiful woman—his mistress, Agnes Sorel—who influenced him greatly in these major positive actions.

In France toward the end of the Hundred Years War, peasants were once again reaping the riches of the fertile soil and builders were beginning to repair the damage inflicted by generations of invading British armies. The conflict had lasted well over one hundred years, from 1337 until 1465, but hope for a permanent peace between England and France seemed about to become reality, and the French King Charles V could at last indulge his passion for building. Having renovated the Louvre and built the Bastille and the splendid Palace of Saint Paul, he dreamed of creating hundreds of gardens and new roads as part of a grand scheme to restore order and beauty to French life. An intellectual who preferred diplomacy to warfare, a patron of the arts, and a collector of books, the widowed Charles V, third king of the Valois line, was known as Charles the Wise. His collection of 917 volumes and thousands of manuscripts became the nucleus of what is today the Bibliothèque Nationale in Paris. He reestablished the authority of the French throne and created a new form of kingship in France in which the king was the peacemaker, the descendant of Charlemagne, a priestly and erudite gentleman. Had Charles the Wise remained King of France for a longer reign, French history might have been altogether different. Unfortunately, in the fifteenth year of his rule, in September 1380, the frail and sickly Charles V died at the age of forty-three. His early death was the beginning of the end of a dream of a peaceful and prosperous France for quite some time.

King Charles V was succeeded by his eldest son, Charles VI, but the new king was only twelve years old at the time of his father's death, so his three paternal uncles—the Dukes of Anjou, Berry, and Burgundy—ruled jointly as co-regents. They did, perhaps, work jointly but also incohesively, with one raising taxes, another quelling sporadic minor rebellions with overzealous soldiers, and the third restricting the power of the nobility. The internal struggle for dominance between the brothers as regent–dukes created tensions within the kingdom that divided the nobility and alarmed the people; the weary population was soon lost in the confusion created by the three unpopular and independent rulers. The masses could respect the authority of one king, even a very young one, but the three discordant royal uncles created civil havoc.

Havoc turned to mayhem, and mayhem became anarchy practically overnight following the stunning impact of the massacre of hundreds of rioters protesting against higher taxes in front of the Hotel de Ville in Paris the night of February 24, 1382. Finally, what should have been the peaceful aftermath of the terrible Hundred Years War coincided with the beginning of the Civil War in France, and during the ensuing seventy long, devastating years of violence, France was a broken and divided country. This early and potent civil strife could have been avoided had the three regent–dukes used foresight, or, lacking foresight, at least observed the previous king's carefully worded regulations governing their regency. Charles V had had a propensity for writing ordinances of all kinds, from coronation ceremonies and royal entries into principal cities to the minutiae of daily court life. Knowing himself to be in poor health, he had not neglected to prepare the way for his young successor, and well before his death he had meticulously pre-ordered the first years of the reign of his son. King Charles VI would be crowned according to the detailed plan his father had drawn up. The Coronation Ceremony was the guideline for all coronations in France until that of Napoleon.

The twelve year old would only rule in his own name when he turned fourteen with the help of a twelve-man Council of Ministers, all trusted collaborators of Charles the Wise. Having chosen his three brothers as regents to his heir for the two-year interim, Charles V further named his brother, the Duke of Burgundy, and his brother-in-law, the Prince of Bourbon, as tutors to the child king. For the two years of the regency, each man serving the new king was given clear, specific duties and responsibilities by the dying king Charles V; the security of the kingdom thus seemed assured.

While united under the supervision of Charles V the dukes had been able enough administrators of their own duchies; unfortunately, they lost their reason with the advent of their new supreme and unfettered authority. The eldest of the three dukes was the brilliant Louis d'Anjou, who was forty-one at the time of the king's death and who had spent most of his life in military service and had as yet little experience in administrative tasks. His brothers did not take him seriously because Anjou was fanciful by nature, a haughty prince who in his youth had been prone to rashness. He was a remarkable horseman, and as lieutenant general of the Languedoc in the southern part of France, he had been too far removed from events in the capital to have an effective influence on the Parisian ministers of Charles V. All the same, Louis d'Anjou was a shrewd prince whose chief objective was the throne of Naples, which he eventually added to his already vast dominions in the southern and central region of France. He also inherited the titles of King of Sicily, Jerusalem, and Cyprus.

The middle brother, Jean, the Duke of Berry, was a man of unusual character and the least qualified to act as regent. Jean de Berry was the aesthete of the family, an indolent and sensual man of the world who cared little for politics and still less for the people. Forty years old when Charles V died, his chief occupations had been amassing and enlarging a vast art collection and embellishing his countless chateaux. The epicurean co-regent had no taste for politics other than as a means of enriching his personal treasury.

Philip, the Duke of Burgundy, later called Philip the Hardy, had none of the weaknesses of the Duke of Berry and was far more ambitious than Louis, the Duke d'Anjou. A soldier and astute administrator, Burgundy was above all a cunning politician. Only thirty-eight when he became co-regent and guardian of his nephew, he was, through his marriage, his independent alliances, and driving ambition, to threaten the very existence of the Valois throne to which he owed his heritage.

Divided into two parts, a duchy and a county, Burgundy for centuries had been a semi-independent realm traditionally loyal to the French throne. In 1361 the duchy of Burgundy was formally united to the French crown by the Valois King John II[1] and granted by him to his youngest son, who thereupon became Duke of Burgundy. The other part of Burgundy, the county, was given to the Count of Flanders and was known as the Franche-Comté. The young duke received immense revenues from the duchy, even then one of the richest regions of France with its lucrative productions of wine, wool, and grains. As if that weren't enough, in 1369 Philip the Hardy married Margaret, the broth-

---

[1] Father of Charles V.

erless daughter of the rich and powerful Count of Flanders. Upon the death of his father-in-law in 1384 the Duke of Burgundy inherited what is today much of Holland, all of Belgium, the Franche-Comté, and most of northern France. As rich as any king and richer by far than any other French prince of the blood, the Duke of Burgundy was the equivalent of a head of state with his own diplomatic corps, treasury, administration, army, and royal court. From his birth as the third son of a struggling king, the Duke of Burgundy had become the most powerful prince in Europe.

Personal ambitions temporarily set aside, the three uncles coordinated the preparations for the coronation and sacrament of the young king. According to the tradition that dated from the fifth century coronation of King Clovis, Charles VI, the fourth Valois King of France, was crowned and anointed in the cathedral of Reims on November 3, 1380. His father had planned every step of the coronation. Not yet thirteen, understanding little in politics, and easily distracted from serious subjects, the young Charles VI was hardly precocious; he enjoyed the trumpets and the splendor of the celebration, so he was more like a child than a king.

During the state banquet following the coronation the uncles Anjou and Burgundy quarreled over the place of honor at the right of the king; the Duke of Anjou claimed the right of seniority as the eldest, and the Duke of Burgundy claimed it as the Premier Peer of France. It was up to young Charles VI to choose; silently he pointed, indicating the vainglorious Duke of Burgundy and thus unwittingly plunged France into a civil war that would long outlast his lifetime. Unfit to rule, King Charles VI would spend his whole adult life mentally detached from the throne. Delirium alternated with bouts of extreme apathy to cloud his view of the realm to an opaque blur.

The eventual reunification of France and her first steps toward the glorious renaissance well under way in other corners of Europe are credited to one of the unlikeliest of men: the malingering and melancholic King Charles VII. Actually, history credits him, but it was undoubtedly his mistress, Agnes Sorel, who saved France.

Said to be the most beautiful woman of her time, and perhaps all time, Agnes Sorel combined beauty and intelligence to the highest degree, and it is thanks to her persistent encouragement and good counsel that the taciturn and apathetic Charles VII had at least a period of awakening, entirely coincidental with their six years together. When they first met, in 1444, he was despondent, mistrusting, and practically powerless; at her premature death in 1450 he had become the Most Christian and Very Victorious King in the Whole of France.

PARIS IN THOSE DAYS

Paris has always been nestled in a basin on both sides of the River Seine and surrounded in every direction by hills and higher ground. In 1400 a visitor to the city would have had a commanding view of all of Paris from the vantage point of Montmartre, then nothing but high hill covered with convents, orchards, and acres of terraced vineyards. Looking down on the city, one's eyes would follow the ribbon of river snaking its path all the way to the distant hamlets of Passy and Auteuil and still farther to St. Cloud. The Seine was much as one sees it today, changing its course every few hundred feet and offering miles of then grassy embankments for promenades, children's games, and fishing.

Jutting straight up, much higher than the great plane and chestnut and elm trees plentiful on the river's banks and beyond, were the twin square towers of the Cathedral of Notre Dame, completed just 35 years earlier on the Ile de la Cité. Still higher was the nearby spire of the Sainte Chapelle, that masterpiece of classic Gothic architecture, completed in 1248, with its collection of holy relics. On both sides of the Seine one could see the turrets of the Louvre; the spires and towers of the Left Bank Abbeys; orchards and great walled-in gardens; and wide crossroads and busy marketplaces, such as Les Halles, creating the feeling of space and light.

Paris at its beginning in the third century BC was situated on two islands and inhabited by the Parissi tribesmen. With the arrival of the Romans in 52 BC the city spread to what is now the Quartier Latin on the Left Bank, was renamed Lutece, and remained the Roman regional capital for 500 years. One can still visit the ruins of a Roman bath just off the Boulevard de Saint Germain, and much of the sophisticated Roman water system is still intact. Under the conquering Frankish King Clovis at the beginning of the sixth century, Paris became the capital of Gaul; then a century later the city lost some of its importance when the Merovingian kings and then the Carolingians centered their activities farther to the south. Charlemagne, after his coronation in Rome on Christmas Day in the year 800, considered Aix-en-Chapelle his favorite residence, yet continued his practice of moving from one city to another with his entire court, thus creating a sort of roving capital.

Paris once again became the seat of power with the coronation of Hugues (Hugh) Capet in 987 and remained the capital from those early medieval days, growing into what would by 1400 become the biggest and most populous of all the cities of the West with its 200,000 inhabitants, which was four times more than London at the same epoch. It is not surprising that Paris was so heavily populated because there were 20 million people in France at the time. Bordeaux, Lyon, Toulouse, Marseilles, Arras, and Rouen were all major cities with populations equal to or greater than that of London. The entire population of England was just more than three million.

By the beginning of the fifteenth century Paris had long outgrown its medieval city walls, the most recent of which had been completed by King Philippe-Auguste in about 1220. Walls encircled the islands, and as both banks of the Seine were settled, high walls were built around large areas of the Right Bank with fortified gates at half-mile intervals. The Left Bank settlements had a smaller enclosure and were guarded by a small fortress, the Petit Châtelet. The city extended well beyond the city walls in length, from the Ile St. Louis to the Louvre, and in width two miles on either side of the Seine. Four great fortresses stood imposingly to intimidate the enemy. The oldest one was the formidable Conciergerie on the Ile de la Cité, its grey turrets and high black towers sharing the island with the Cathedral of Notre Dame and its cloisters, the Sainte Chapelle, and the Palace of Justice. The Conciergerie was a royal residence and the meeting place for Parliament. The kings of France held council meetings there in the Great Hall, admired throughout Europe for its Gothic beauty. Prisoners, after sentencing in the adjacent Palace of Justice, were led down the stone stairs to the grimy damp dungeons to await their fate.

Across the Seine on the Right Bank and to the north stood the Bastille, recently built by Charles V. Although the Bastille figured often in French history, beginning with an uprising in the early fifteenth century, it was actually a rather small, moated fortress with one drawbridge. It could hold only 350 prisoners or so and was intended for political prisoners, not common criminals.

In contrast, the great grim fortress of the Grand Châtelet appeared to contain an army of ogres. Enormous and forbidding, the Grand Châtelet was feared. Its great blackened walls looming on the riverside were a constant reminder of the fort's prison and torture chambers within.

The fourth fortress of Paris was the square, crenellated Louvre, defending the city's west entrance. Built in 1220 by Philippe-Auguste, the great royal builder, it was a simple crusader's castle with cramped royal apartments. It was surrounded by a deep moat and intended chiefly for defense.

In 1400, as for centuries before and since, the River Seine was the heart and soul of Paris. It is one of Europe's great rivers, nearly 500 miles long from birth in the highlands of Burgundy. It winds its serpentine way to the northern French coast and then into the English Channel. The Seine rises at 1,545 feet, traveling northwest through Champagne country before looping lazily west to enter the Ile-de-France. At Montereau it receives the Yonne and turns north toward Paris, where it is joined by its great tributary the Marne. Then it flows gently through the Paris Basin at only 80 feet above sea level. Once on the other side of Paris the Seine has completed roughly half of its course and picks up the Oise for the rest of its life in the meandering northwesterly course toward the sea. On its way it passes through Rouen, a medieval port of major importance, before reaching the great deep-water port of Le Havre and finally the Channel. The Seine is a friendly river, perfectly navigable, never rushing, not too wide, and yet deep enough to allow vessels drawing ten feet to dock at the quays of Paris.

In 1400, goods arrived by the ton day and night, were unloaded onto the quays, and were distributed quickly to the city's numerous marketplaces. Wood, wheat, drums of oil, fish, bolts of cloth, salt, candles, wine, meat, and produce were plentiful, and the streets of Paris were a beehive of activity, with shops, stalls, and carts up and down every street.

The Marais on the Right Bank was the commercial center of Paris. It is here, too, that the royal palaces stood, with the great hotels of the nobles nearby. The vast Hôtel Saint Paul with its annex the Hôtel Petit-y-Musc, the Hôtel des Tournelles, and the queen's Hotel Barbette—all splendid palaces—were cheek by jowl beside the houses of merchants, shopkeepers, and common folk. The streets were narrow, unpaved, and littered with filth, and the noisy commotion of street life was incessant. To the clamor of vendors hawking their wares was added the sounds of children playing, horse hooves, clanging metal, and pealing bells from the dozens of churches of the Marais. Every two streets had a church and they all rang to announce the call to mass; on holidays the thousands of bells pealed continuously from dawn to dusk.

The nobles gathered in their great mansions, the beggars sprawled on church steps and near the taverns, shopkeepers guarded their shops, and the priests kept busy in their parishes, but they all rubbed shoulders in the tiny streets of Paris. The gathering place was the Place de Grève in front of the

Hotel de Ville, then called the House of Pillars (Maison aux Piliers) and the first of the three city halls built on the present site. Here was a microcosm of Paris. Sometimes the crowds swelled in numbers and protested boisterously, usually against an increase in taxes; sometimes the protests led to bloodshed. Most often the Place de Grève was a lively square filled with jugglers and acrobats and musicians and vendors selling sweet meats and beignets and wine.

Paris by night was another scene altogether. Shutters and doors were locked tight, streetlamps were rare, and the maze of bustling streets became eerily silent and empty. The night's activities belonged to the thieves, beggars, and prostitutes and to the dogs and cats poking through the rubbish.

At the beginning of the twelfth century a theology professor at the Cathedral Notre Dame crossed over to the Left Bank and set up an outdoor school of thought near the present-day Place Maubert. His name was Abelard and he is much better known for the tragic romance with Heloïse than for matters of church doctrine. It was a group of his followers, however, who won the right in 1200 from both the king and the pope to govern their own community. This was the birth of the University of Paris. Established on the Left Bank, the members of the council of the University of Paris were to become politically powerful. The Sorbonne was founded at about the same time and the Left Bank became synonymous with intellect, a notion that exists to this day. The church was the biggest landowner on the opposite side of the Seine from the royal palaces and the city hall; now freed from all restraint, the church ran the Left Bank as if it were the Vatican itself. Greedy and ambitious priests and bishops vied with each other for power and glory with all the fine accompaniments, and the common people were all but forgotten.

Power structure is best represented by a pyramid: At the top of the pyramid of course was the king and his court, including the army or what served as an army (a real standing army did not exist in 1400). The second thin strata was made up of the nobles and their court. A close third would be the University of Paris because the clerics held great power in the capital. The fourth group comprised the members of the guilds: the artisans, grocers, and tradesmen. Of these guildsmen, the butchers were by far the most important—they were the biggest, the strongest, the richest, and the loudest and held sway with the masses. The butchers and their assistants, the "écorcheurs" or skinners, would play a major role in the Civil War of the fifteenth century. At the bottom of the pyramid, as always, we find the poor, the peasants, laborers, and the little people. As always, they would suffer the most.

CHAPTER ONE

At the turn of the fifteenth century most of France, and especially Paris, was a sea of immorality. The feudal system was coming apart at the seams and the overtaxed nobility was no longer able to feed their peasants. Thousands upon thousands of rural families swarmed into overcrowded cities seeking food, which was scarce, and shelter. Incest, bigamy, and murder were common and human lives counted for little. In 1409 in Paris on one night alone, 519 murders were reported between the rue St. Antoine and the rue du Roi de Sicile, an area of about one tenth of a square mile. Corruption was a way of life, government was erratic, and very few people expected spiritual or material aid from the church, itself a jungle of power-hungry clerics who had strayed far from their faith. The church was in the midst of a great schism and had two popes simultaneously: a pope in Rome and one in Avignon who had never been a priest. He was replaced by a Spaniard, Pedro de Luna, who had once been a pirate. Eventually, even a third pope appeared briefly out of the chaos which was fourteenth and fifteenth century Christianity. This was at a time when the forces of Islam, united under Turkish banners, were preparing to conquer Eastern Europe!

In Paris many people showed open reverence for the devil, entire families were beginning to die of starvation, and loud wailing could be heard all over the city day and night. It was into this tragic epoch that poor little Charles Valois was born.

Charles VI married Isabel, of Bavaria, on July 13, 1385, in the Cathedral of Amiens. He was then seventeen years old. When young, he had distinguished himself as a knight of brave character in battles in Normandy and

Flanders. Sadly, he was to develop mental illness, which affected his long reign. The queen, fat and flamboyant, forgot her husband amid pleasures and dances; she gave receptions and lived in total debauchery. Early into her husband's reign, she had allied herself with the Burgundians, long feudal enemies of the Valois.

Young Charles's birth could hardly have been more unrelated to destiny. Born on a dark morning in Paris in the royal palace of Saint Paul, February 22, 1403, he was the eleventh child and fifth son of a madwoman who was queen of France. Within hours of his birth the small and sickly baby was christened Charles de Valois, given the title of Count of Ponthieu, and sent to live on the banks of the Seine in an annex of the royal residence. His mother then renewed her raucous and debauched life.

The queen had an excessive lust for opulence in any form and she was insatiable in every respect, a trait that increased in intensity as she grew into middle age. Having given birth to another royal child meant little more to her than the gifts she would be able to extricate from the king: another chateau, a rich abbey, or other productive domains. Queen Isabel spent money without restraint and collected everything, amassing furs, jewels, silver and gold objects, furniture, and tapestries. In her vast apartments, virtually littered with her treasures, dozens of exotic birds flew about freely, and she kept a tame leopard by her side. But her special predilection was for young men.

Isabel was born in Germany in 1370. Her father, Duke Stephen II of Bavaria, was a Wittelsbach prince and her mother was a Visconti from Milan. Less than five feet tall, olive skinned, and black eyed, Isabel eventually became monstrously obese to the point of being unable to walk. She was an undeterred and outrageous nymphomaniac until the end of her life, and as an old woman she would be carried to her window to sit, beckoning young strangers to come up to her room and into her bed. But as a young bride of fifteen she was energetic, pretty, festive, and gay, and the beginning of her marriage to Charles VI in 1385 was a happy one. The Duke of Normandy had arranged the marriage agreement between his nephew and the little princess from Munich, and their first meeting took place at Amiens on July 10, 1385. Burgundy had planned for the marriage to follow some time during the autumn, but such was the overwhelming attraction between the two adolescents that they pressed for an immediate wedding. Oblivious to the protests of his uncle, King Charles VI married Isabel of Bavaria eight days after their first encounter in a hastily organized wedding celebrated in the Cathedral of Amiens. With their wedding feast they inaugurated a life of uninterrupted balls and banquets, mimes and masques that would last the next seven years.

Only seventeen when they married, Charles VI was tall, blond, chivalrous, and attractive, and he had already distinguished himself as a soldier. The peace with England was fragile but holding, and in spite of the rumbling and grumbling of the population over taxes, the early years of his rule promised good things. At the time of Isabel's coronation in the Sainte-Chapelle in 1389 the royal couple was hugely popular, particularly with the masses, and their progression throughout the Ile de France in the autumn of the same year gave occasion for fêtes and fireworks everywhere they went. It was a promising change for the people after the severity of the plagues, famine, and wars, which had marred most of the previous 150 years.

Charles VI, as a child king, had chosen the sun as his emblem, thus preceding Louis XIV by two and a half centuries. It was to be the only thing they had in common. The first Sun King suffered from severe mental illness, which was undiagnosed in his youth but became progressively apparent with age. At the time of his marriage, although his schizophrenia was becoming evident to some, it was generally misconstrued as simply bad temper and mental apathy. In 1392, however, he was seized with a sudden attack of total madness in Le Mans and, turning on his own men, he killed one soldier and wounded many others with his own sword. Coming to his senses for a brief instant, he realized what he had done, which brought on another fit. Within days the king's insanity would become known to all: Lashed to a simple wooden cart drawn by a pair of oxen, the King of France, only twenty-four years old, was brought back to Paris, never to regain his sanity, an allegorical sunset on the house of Valois. Until his death in 1435 he had only occasional and brief contact with reality.

Isolated by his uncles, during his attacks Charles VI was locked up in the Louvre or the Hotel Saint Paul where he spent weeks at a time tearing up his clothes, smashing furniture into very small pieces, and refusing to eat because he imagined that his food was poisoned. Weak from malnutrition, unwashed, and his naked body covered with lice, he repeatedly proclaimed that he was no longer to be called Charles VI but King George the Wounded.

He developed a loathing for the frivolous Isabel, and during his increasingly frequent lapses from sanity he hurled any object within reach and screamed lunatic abuse at the queen or anyone else within a convenient distance. The royal family, no more enlightened than anyone else at the time as to how to deal with mental illness, actually tried to cure the king by bringing him madwomen for company. At first the only person who could calm him during his rages was his sister-in-law, the sweet and pious Valentine, Duchess of Orléans. In later years he loved the daughter of a wigmaker, Odile de Champvilliers, who taught him to play card games, a new fad at the time, and read tarot cards; these were the only pastimes he enjoyed. Odile alone remained steadfastly close to the king until his death thirty years later, and she bore him a daughter.

While the king drew appeasing comfort from the visits of the Duchess of Orléans, the queen threw herself into the arms of the Duke of Orléans, Charles's younger brother. Louis d'Orléans, rakish, handsome, and witty, was a notorious ladies' man and gambler and was widely criticized for his outrageous expenses of tens of thousands of gold francs a day. His dining room walls were hung with dozens of portraits of his past and present mistresses, and it gave the boorish duke the greatest pleasure to invite the ladies' husbands to dine with him there. An experienced voluptuary, Louis was the epitome of licentiousness, and the silly queen adopted his ways with unbridled enthusiasm.

The Duke of Orléans was, however, politically ambitious; before his brother's madness became public knowledge he resolved to become sole regent and advised his uncles that he no longer considered their tutelage necessary. For the next few years he actually ruled France with the help of his father's old ministers, called derisively the Marmousets.[2] A quarrel with his Uncle Burgundy in 1404 became an issue that was to erupt immediately into civil strife in Paris; within five years most of France was divided in loyalties and the countryside would be laid to ruin once again.

---

[2] As its origin "marmot" meant "petite figure grotesque" (small grotesque person).

CHAPTER TWO

The royal annex, a dependency of the enormous palace of Saint Paul, was a grim Hôtel Pute-y-Musse, better known as the Petit-Musc. The tiny Prince Charles, only hours old, was taken there to join the boisterous household where his two brothers and a sister lived. He was given over to the care of a wet nurse, Joan Chamoisy, and a governess, Joan de Mesnil, who were to be his only comfort and security during the sad years that lay ahead.

The baby Count de Ponthieu did not want for material comfort and had all the furnishings, clothes, and toys a royal youngster of the early fifteenth century might be expected to have. The palace inventory lists Charles's painted cradle of Irish wood and a matching wooden screen; also new blinds were put on his windows to protect him from drafts, and he played with wooden animals, metal boxes, and silver pots. All the Valois children had extensive wardrobes and received new clothes for Christmas, Easter, and other feast days; as a baby Charles wore a scarlet mantel, embroidered waistcoats, plumed velvet caps, and a gold belt.

His christening was a solemn ceremony attended by both his parents, King Charles VI being temporarily lucid. His godparents were the Constable Charles d'Albret, the Count of Luyrieux, and Joan of Luxembourg. From then on he was given over to his own loving nurses, the Joans of the nursery, who gave him the warmth and attention a small child needs, rocked his cradle for hours, sang soothing lullabies to the accompaniment of the harp in his room, and tried to shield him from the ever-present brutalities of the day.

His brothers and sisters were hardly companions for the baby. Two boys and a girl had already died before the birth of Charles, and three other girls, upon reaching the age of eight, had married and lived far from Petit-Musc. Isabel, born in 1389, was the little queen of Richard II of England; after his death in 1399, she would then marry Charles, the eldest son of the Duke of Orléans, and die in childbirth at the age of twenty. Joan, eleven years older than Charles, was married to the Duke of Brittanny. Michele was married to Philip the Good of Burgundy, the grandson of the formidable Duke of Burgundy, Philip the Hardy. She had been taken as a young girl to be raised in Flanders. Born in 1395, Michele would die in 1422, a Burgundian until the end. A fourth sister, Marie, had entered the church in childhood and lived by her father's side, determined to cure him of his insanity through prayer. She too would die young. The only ones left in the annex with Charles were his eldest brother, the Dauphin Louis, born in 1397; the middle brother John, Count of Touraine, born in 1398; and Catherine, two years older than Charles. Catherine would one day marry the Lancastrian King Henry V of England and, widowed in 1422, would thereupon wed Owen Tudor, founder of the long-lasting Tudor dynasty.

Since even before the birth of the smallest Valois there had been doubt as to his legitimacy, a stigma that plagued Charles until he was a grown man and king. His doubts were finally put to rest in 1429 when, as the troubled Charles VII, he met face-to-face with Joan of Arc and she publicly proclaimed him to be the son and heir of Charles VI. His own mother didn't help at all, alternately claiming from Charles's youth until the end of her own life that he was or was not the son of the king, as it suited her political interests. Generally it was thought that he was the bastard son of his uncle, Louis d'Orléans. Many French historians are inclined to think that Charles was, in fact, the legitimate son of the king, the chief reason being that Queen Isabel rarely showed the slightest interest in any of her first eleven children but was openly very excited about the birth of her twelfth child, Philip, her "love child" as she called him and thought to be the son of the Duke of Orléans. She was utterly disconsolate when the baby died just a few days after his birth. Conjugal visits to the king during his occasional periods of normal behavior were expected of her as queen, and one must assume her first eleven children were indeed legitimate offspring of Charles VI. In any case they were all officially recognized as such. Charles only rarely saw his mother; Isabel was totally engulfed in her own pleasures.

The queen did not try to hide her affair with the Duke of Orléans; if anything she flaunted it, joining him in his dissolute existence and openly favoring his ambitions to rule. He had the good looks and charm of his brother; although intelligent, he had lost his sense of judgment in his lust for power. Taking full advantage of the king's dementia, Orléans added to his possessions, which were manifold. Besides the county of Asti in Italy, which had come to him through his wife's dowry, the Duchies of Luxembourg and Orlé-ans were his, as were the counties of Perigord, Angoulême, Blois, Dreux, Soisson, and other counties and innumerable seigneuries.

In April 1404, the aging Uncle Philip, Duke of Burgundy, fell ill and took to bed; three weeks later, on April 25, he died. Succeeded by his son John as Duke of Burgundy and Count of Flanders, the legendary duke was buried with great pomp in the grandiose chartreuse of Champmol near Dijon in Burgundy.

The young Duke John of Burgundy was very different from his glamorous father. He was short and ugly, with an overly large head, and he was unrefined, inelegant, and cruel. Ambitious to the extreme, he nevertheless retired to his palaces in Flanders and remained far from Paris for more than a year. His year of mourning over and his administration in order, he returned to Paris, anxious to claim his father's seat on the council and renew the Burgundian thrust for power.

The rising fortunes of the Duke of Orléans presented a threat to his ambitious cousin John of Burgundy, and the new Duke of Burgundy soon made it clear that he himself would rule—alone. By this time the Duke of Berry was in poor health, and the moderate Duke of Anjou, who was also King of Naples and Sicily, spent most of his time in the south, far from the intrigues in the capital. The jockeying for political power in the royal family was slow in coming to a complete rupture, but in 1406, when the inevitable rupture broke, it was sudden and Paris was in a state of great alarm. The city, more and more densely populated, filthy, and alive with activity round the clock, was suddenly invaded with thousands of armed supporters of Orléans and an equally strong private army loyal to the Duke of Burgundy.

These belligerent, armed men on the loose killed each other whenever they met, more often than not wounding or taking lives of the innocent who happened to be in the vicinity. The cries of the dying and wounded added to the din of the already congested streets. The Seine was littered with hundreds of floating dead bodies, disease became rampant, and no one was safe, not even the rich or the royal. Children were not protected, and Charles, even behind the thick walls of the Petit-Musc, was no exception. In spite of the efforts of the two Joans, he could not be screened from the blasphemous, ribald, ugly, and dangerous life around him. At the tender age of three, he was gathered hastily in the middle of the night and carried to a rowboat in the Seine, which slipped away through the dark and foul-smelling waters. The object of their fear and flight, the mighty Burgundy duke, was leading a massive attack on Paris. The terrified band of royal escapees didn't get very far. Captured by the Burgundians, they were returned to the Petit-Musc and kept under house arrest with no one to turn to for help. There they remained for a year.

The following year, 1407, was worse still. After a second failed attempt to flee Paris and the Burgundian soldiers, the Valois children learned of the murder of their Uncle Louis of Orléans.

Queen Isabel had bought her own grand house, part of which still stands at the corner of the rue Vieille-du-Temple and the rue Barbette, and had a court all her own, totally separate from those of the Hotel Saint Paul and the Louvre. Here in the Hotel Barbette she lived in wanton luxury, immune to the starving, howling poor outside her doors and impervious to the political catastrophe swirling about her family and the throne.

It was upon leaving this house in the rue Barbette that the Duke of Orléans was assassinated at about eight o'clock on November 23, 1407. Paris was under curfew and the streets were nearly empty when the duke, on foot and accompanied only by four torch bearers and four men on horseback, was attacked by a small band of Burgundy's men. Strangled to death, his head was then cut off; dripping blood, it was impaled on a lance for all to see, lit by torchlight during the night, and raised high above the crowds the next day so that everyone could get a look at the enemy of John the Fearless, as the young Duke of Burgundy was known. Then the mutilated body of the once handsome Duke of Orléans was transported to his palace, and the funeral was held the following day at the church of the Blancs-Manteaux. The Duke of Burgundy, dressed in deep mourning, attended the services, affecting great distress over the death of his cousin.

Of course, the murderer of the brother of the King of France could not go unpunished. Fingers were pointed in all directions; jealous husbands of former mistresses were brought to court. Even Valentine Visconti, the pious widow of Louis d'Orléans, was accused of having had her husband murdered. Fearful of the consequences, no one dared to implicate the Duke of Burgundy as perpetrator of the crime until he himself publicly claimed responsibility for the murder one month later. He then immediately seized the government and kept the royal family hostage in their respective residences. The city was his.

King Charles VI, who had no idea that he was under arrest, was not even dimly aware of the dire circumstances threatening his family and the throne and remained in his apartments as usual. The Duke of Burgundy paid frequent visits to the palace, giving the king ordinances and decrees to sign; even in his demented state, Charles VI was still the rightful king of France, and his signature assured the legality of Burgundy's every action.

The witless Queen Isabel, hysterical at first and fearing for her own life after the murder of her lover, sent urgent messages to the Burgundian duke, assuring him of her devotion to his cause. This was to be the first of countless instances in which Isabel would change loyalties overnight. The wily duke took full advantage of the queen's stupidity by naming her regent; knowing her to be incapable of negotiation or of making the least decision pertinent to the throne, he thus gained a potentially useful pawn with which to further his own interests. Within months of the murder of the Duke of Orléans Burgundy had become the undisputed dictator of France. To consolidate his authority he named himself sole guardian of the twelve-year-old Dauphin Louis, who was then engaged to Burgundy's own daughter, Margaret.

The de facto rule of the Duke of Burgundy had lasted nearly two years without any new opposition; he had become overconfident. His uncles were preoccupied with their own provinces and were far from Paris, he held the helpless royal family in the palm of his hand, and there was no reason to believe that his rule could not last forever.

But in his conceit he had overlooked the power of vengeance, and he had underestimated his young cousin the poet, Charles, the new Duke of Orléans. Charles and his younger brother John had left Paris after the death of their father and had gone to the Loire Valley to live with their mother, Valentine, in Blois. Resolved to vindicate his father's death and to protect the throne of France from the megalomaniac Duke of Burgundy, Charles of Orléans met secretly with one after the other of those princes of the blood, dukes, and other powerful nobles whom he thought had a reason to wish for the end of the Burgundian dictatorship. They were many and they met in Gien in April 1410. Besides the Orléans brothers the principal participants were the Duke of Berry and Bourbon; the Duke of Alençon; the Duke of the independent Duchy of Britanny; and a forceful Gascon warlord from southwestern France, Bernard, the Count of Armagnac. They all agreed to unite their forces under the leadership of the feisty Count of Armagnac; thereafter, partisans of the Orléans alliance would be known as Armagnacs. The issue of this meeting was that the country would soon be engulfed in civil war, putting the Burgundian north against the Royalist south, civil servants against scholars, and the masses against the already divided nobility.

Another outcome of the meeting was an alliance within an alliance: Recently widowed by the death in childbirth of his twenty-year-old wife Isabel of France (a daughter of Charles VI and herself the widow of Richard II of England), the Duke of Orléans was engaged to Bonne, the daughter of the Count of Armagnac. Thus the somber meeting adjourned on a cheerful note.

Upon hearing of the Armagnac coalition the Duke of Burgundy, who was unprepared for such a threat, hastily called on his allies for support. He even had King Charles VI sign a royal decree outlawing the Royalist movement. After several tentative efforts to call a truce, it was evident that war was inevitable. Armagnac had been gathering and preparing his army for months and by the summer of 1411 had begun to march north toward Paris, the bloodthirsty and boisterous Armagnacs massacring everyone along their way who did not show support for their standard, a plain white flag. Arriving at the gates of Paris they had little trouble penetrating the city, and after a few days of bloody battle they proved themselves to be the stronger force.

The Duke of Burgundy, so long the dominant political personality and unwilling to face defeat, called on King Henry IV of England for help. The English king, finally secure on his usurped throne, was convinced by his ministers to intercede; assured that he held the hereditary Plantagenet claim to rule France he immediately dispatched nine thousand English troops under the command of the Earl of Arundel across the Channel. A quarter of a century after the end of the Hundred Years War the magnificent English archers, this time with the red cross of the House of Lancaster blazing on their armor, were once again marching across the French countryside. Armagnac and his men were forced to retreat in the face of this new and formidable enemy, first to Poitiers and then to Bourges in the center of France, where they were obliged to sign a temporary peace treaty with the Duke of Burgundy and his new allies.

But the Lancastrian King Henry IV was suffering from leprosy and he died on March 20, 1413 and was buried in Westminster Abbey. His son and successor, the dazzling Henry V, wished to concentrate his efforts on domestic policy for the time being and, temporarily retiring from foreign affairs, called his English troops home.

France was left in a state of uneasy calm. The French royal family, misguided and disunited, vacillated in their allegiance to Burgundy or to Armagnac. The young Dauphin Louis, now sixteen, thought of nothing but dances and women, and the queen was behaving scandalously, openly consorting with a succession of young men. A lunatic king, an undignified queen,, and a frivolous dauphin combined to fuel the combustive masses into a spontaneous explosion of fear and panic, and on the night of May 3, 1413, large angry mobs roamed the streets unchecked and stormed the Bastille, the first of countless attacks on the massive prison fortress that would punctuate centuries of French history.

Prisoners by the hundreds, released by the mobs, were masters of the streets. The most unruly of the newly free, elated by their sense of power, actually entered the dauphin's quarters in the Louvre and took some twenty of his officers and men, tied them up, and threw them into the Seine to drown. The Dauphin Louis himself was spared, but his experience and the violence in the Paris streets had shaken the royal family and its court to the core. Even the mighty Duke of Burgundy fled the anarchy in the city, taking the king and queen with him.

The other members of the House of Valois gathered hastily in Pontoise about ten miles northwest of Paris for an emergency meeting, a council dominated by the skillful Duke of Anjou and his intelligent wife, Yolande of Aragon. Of those who had any influence at all within the royal house of France, the Anjous were the most resolute and the most objective and offered the royal cause its only wise counsel: absolute independence from foreign—that is, English—domination. The Duke of Burgundy was thus clearly indicated once more as the principal enemy of France.

CHAPTER THREE

During these tempestuous days of heated discussion, the subtle and ingenious Yolande arranged to meet secretly with Queen Isabel. On the October 21, 1413, the two cousins, one ostentatiously overdressed and the other majestic and collected, met about twenty miles south of Paris at the Chateau de Marcoussis to discuss the possibility of marriage between two of their royal offspring.

Charles was ten years old, and his two elder brothers were already married: Louis the dauphin to the Duke of Burgundy's daughter Margaret and John to Jacqueline de Bavaria-Hainaut, a niece of the Duchess of Burgundy. Charles's sister Joan was married to the eldest son of the Burgundy duke. To Yolande's patriotic mind, there were too many members of the royal Valois family aligned to the Burgundian house.

The Duke and Duchess of Anjou finalized the rupture with the House of Burgundy by breaking the engagement of their eldest son with the daughter of the Duke of Burgundy, promptly sending young Catherine of Burgundy home to Flanders. A week later at Queen Isabel's private residence in the rue Barbette, the two mothers agreed that the youngest Valois prince would marry little Marie of Anjou, born October 14, 1404 and just a year younger than Charles. The engagement celebrations honoring these two royal children began almost immediately with a series of feasts, balls, and jousts held at the Louvre in spite of the political chaos about them. Charles was ten years old, and Marie was just nine.

The damp, dark winter months in Paris did not agree with the Duke and Duchess of Anjou, who longed to return south to the Loire Valley. Not wanting to separate the young couple, Yolande asked and received permission from the indifferent Isabel to take Charles with them to Angers, the capital of Anjou. So, on February 5, 1414, the slight and ungainly Charles, who had just turned eleven years old, began his journey, quitting the noise, stench, and dangers of Paris and leaving behind his wild mother and the poor terrified Charles VI, who was more than ever plagued with demons. He would not miss his parents because he seldom saw them anyway, and when they did meet it was unpleasant for Charles. During one rare interview with his father, the king asked Charles how long it had been since he had last seen his mother. "Three months, sir," he replied.

Yolande of Anjou had become fond of the frail and mistrusting little boy and she became his guide and mentor, even a mother to him. Her kindness and clarity of mind warmed his warped soul and he began to feel almost secure; perhaps it was too late to undo the damage of his first pathetic years, but at last Charles had entered into a normal family life. Yolande and Louis II had five children: Louis, Marie, René, Yolande, and a Charles of their own. Charles de Valois became, for all practical purposes, the sixth child of this extraordinary couple and for the rest of his life he considered the five Anjou cousins to be his own brothers and sisters.

When in her mid-thirties, Yolande of Anjou, Queen of Sicily, "adopted" Charles. She was born a princess of Aragon, the daughter of King John I, and the head of the royal house in eastern Spain so long at odds, and sometimes at war, with the house of Anjou, its neighbor across the Pyrénées. The beautiful and regal princess was at first devastated to learn that her fate would be marriage to the heir of the throne of the Angevin enemies. Once decided that only she could bring peace to the two warring houses, however, she entered into her new role with her customary zeal and intelligence. As King of Sicily, Louis II, Duke of Anjou was the titular head of an enormous heritage that included, besides Anjou and Sicily, Provence, Maine, Guise, Naples, and eventually the Lorraine. He also was pretender to the thrones of Cyprus and Jerusalem, Majorca, and the Roussillon, which is today the Côte d'Azur and the Maritime Alps. At their marriage in Arles, on December 2, 1400, the twenty-three-year-old Louis fell instantly in love with his bride and their marriage, purely political by arrangement, became one of the outstanding unions in history, loving and devoted and with great intellectual complicity. Yolande was the cool-headed politician–administrator, and Louis II was the energetic soldier–diplomat.

Their chateau at Angers, still standing intact, an immense crenelated red brick fortress with eighteen formidable towers and magnificent gardens, became home to Charles, who had known only the noisy and crowded Petit-Musc. Here in the Anjou household, Charles discovered a warm and affectionate family who lived in a world he could not have imagined. The mild climate, the gentle people, and the sweetness of the Loire Valley must have seemed a veritable Eden to the nervous and sickly boy. He discovered the hills and meandering rivers and the rich brown sun-washed soil with its endless fields of crops and came to love the natural beauty of the countryside, perhaps the prettiest in France. Eventually he would adopt the whole region of the Loire as his own, and for the rest of his life the Loire Valley remained the only part of France where he could feel comfortable.

Charles, since birth a solemn child, had spent most of his miserable youth in a constant state of fear. He was small for his age, with a long sad face and an elongated head. His arms, too, were unusually long for a little boy, and he would never quite grow into them; his legs were short and knock-kneed. He had thin reddish-brown hair, tiny grey–green eyes, and thick lips that turned down at the corners. Although not hideous, Charles, by all accounts, must have been quite an ugly eleven-year-old boy. As he grew older he devised ways of hiding his misshapen legs by wearing his tunics longer than was the style of the age, and he never appeared hatless in public; there is no existing portrait of Charles without a usually rather broad-brimmed embroidered felt hat covering his whole head. Unsmiling and aloof most of his life, he was never to lose the flat and expressionless gaze he had had since early childhood.

But he blossomed in many ways during his two years at Angers under the loving and maternal care of his "bonne mère" Yolande. He studied daily with the tutors of the Anjou children and took an avid interest in all subjects, especially sciences, Latin, and history. From his development of his hitherto neglected mind emerged a latent intelligence that was to make him one of the few intellectual princes of his turbulent epoch.

Although he was withdrawn at first, the youngest Valois, emerging slowly from behind his sullen wall of defense, learned to enjoy children's games and was taught to fence and to ride and quickly caught on to the intricacies of chess. His cousins, accustomed as they were to the pleasant routine of their large and demonstrative family, were kind and patient with the spindly newcomer, and Charles grew to love his new family and his new life. He was especially fond of his "sister" Marie who also was his fiancée. At his tender age Charles felt a brotherly affection for her that would never evolve into anything deeper.

Marie, however, adored her strange cousin and was to remain devotedly in love with him for all her long life. Marie was tiny, intelligent, pretty, and pious and would prove her infinite inner strength over and over again during their arduous years ahead.

Women were always to wield the greatest influence over Charles; they were his mainstay, supporting him throughout a lifetime of problems of catastrophic proportions, both on the human and the national scale. The two affectionate Joans of his childhood, a third Joan, the Maid of Orléans, and his saintly wife Marie were all there when he most needed them. Yolande of Anjou taught him how to be a king; much later his beloved mistress Agnès Sorel encouraged him to act like one. These women were the positive sustaining forces he needed to help him along the tedious and winding path to glory.

Right from birth Charles had little close contact with men, and those he had seen the most frequently at court were lewd and corrupt, thus depriving him of an appropriate male role model. The moral laxity of his early environment must be the chief reason for Charles's lifelong inclination to choose the most dissolute men for companions. Rather like the battered child who, once a parent, beats his own children, Charles, instead of feeling revulsion toward the depraved and their debauchery, was attracted to them and sought their company.

The one man who could have coaxed the sluggish and unconfident future king into promising manhood was his uncle Louis II of Anjou, the King of Sicily. The first member of the royal family to travel extensively, Louis of Anjou was familiar with the cultures and people throughout the Mediterranean basin, from Spain to the Holy Land. He brought back to Angers tantalizing specimens from faraway lands: paintings and sculptures from Italy; rare plants from the Mediterranean islands; and perfumes, spices, silk, mirrors, mosaics, and carpets from the East. Paving the way for the renaissance in France, he introduced artists and poets and musicians into the sunny existence of the Anjou, and he shared with Yolande a keen interest in the education of their children. A wise ruler, accomplished linguist, able administrator, and brave soldier, Louis was the ideal example of character and integrity for the shy, grave young prince. A few more years under the firm guidance of his exceptional uncle may have made the necessary difference to Charles's innate moral lassitude. Tragically, this was not to be.

CHAPTER FOUR

Suddenly, in the late summer of 1415, Charles's happy world came to an abrupt end; fate, in the form of King Henry V of England, had intervened.

King Henry V, the second Lancastrian King of England, was born in 1387, two years after the death of Charles V of France, and began his reign in 1413, half a century after the Hundred Years War had supposedly ended. Later immortalized by William Shakespeare as a reckless and quarrelsome young man who changed overnight when he became king, in fact Henry V was perhaps the most astute and best-educated king of his era. Twenty-six years old, well-prepared to rule, and impatient to succeed his father, Henry V began his reign by mercilessly suppressing his opposition. Finally secure on his throne and tempted by the civil strife in France, the English king then re-launched with missionary zeal the Plantagenet claim to the French throne. Henry V was deeply religious and believed that the conquest of France was a God-given mandate; he said he had to "cure the French of their vices"!

In 1414, he signed a separate peace treaty in Leicester with the Duke of Burgundy in which they agreed not to bear arms against one another. He then sent an embassy to Paris to ask King Charles VI for immediate capitulation. Two months later the French King's Council and Bernard of Armagnac sent an absurdly large—some 600 men—French embassy to England on behalf of Charles VI with a counter-proposal: the hand of Princess Catherine, the youngest daughter of the French king, and part of the Aquitaine. This was a paltry offering—King Henry wanted all of France! The French assumed that the diplomatic dickering would last indefinitely, but the English king was only bartering for time. During the year of half-hearted attempts at diplomacy, while messengers sailed back and forth across the Channel and embassies negotiated, the English army was readying for war.

Generously funded by Parliament and with the enthusiastic support of his subjects, the King of England left Southampton on August 11, 1415 with thirty-thousand soldiers and a fleet of more than twelve hundred ships. By the time Louis of Anjou, the Duke of Burgundy, and Bernard of Armagnac could confer, it was too late. The ruthless English warrior king and his thousands of crack archers had landed at the small port city of Harfleur in Normandy. The leaders of the French factions were stunned into immediate inaction.

The English forces, practically unopposed, laid siege to Harfleur on August 19, and three days later the city was theirs. King Henry then renounced his original plan to march on Paris and, leaving a garrison of ten thousand soldiers at Harfleur, he and his remaining army crossed the Somme in mid-October and headed for Calais.

The French had never had a standing army; it would be created thirty years later by Charles VII. Thus it was left to the Duke of Anjou, the Duke of Orléans, and the Count of Armagnac to organize a fighting force; a desperate call to arms was sent throughout the country. The taciturn Duke of Burgundy, in accordance with the recent Leicester treaty, stood back and watched from a distance while his cousins tried to forge an army. Burgundy's brother, the Duke of Brabant, however, sent a substantial independent Burgundian force to fight on the side of the French. Thousands of independent Royalists came to fight, and Armagnac brought thousands more Gascons. By October the French forces commanded by the Count of Albret (godfather of the future Charles VII) were a poorly organized but spirited and optimistic army of more than fifty-thousand mostly mounted soldiers. The vast majority of this new and inexperienced army was made up of young sons of the nobility and landed gentry from every county in France; few of them had ever seen battle.

The opposing armies met on October 25, 1415, at Agincourt. King Henry's much smaller army devastated the French defenders in a chaotic muddy and bloody massacre that decimated the elite of French youth overnight. The English only lost four hundred men; seven thousand French soldiers died on the narrow battlefield of Agincourt. Nearly two thousand French survivors were taken prisoner, including Charles, the Duke of Orléans and his brother John, the Count of Angoulême and future grandfather of François I. A ditty at the time said, "If you want to see the best of France, you have to go to England!"

The victorious Henry V, having successfully annihilated the Royalists, the independent Burgundians, and the Armagnacs, three enemy forces united for once, then sailed from Calais back to England to plan for a permanent administration in France. He had spent less than three months on the French soil and in just that short time left a shocked and quarreling country in total disarray with no ruler, no government, no army, and no hope. Louis II of Anjou, ever the wise counselor, tried to pick up the pieces and patch what was left of a shattered France. But the Anjou duke's most important task at hand was to diminish the power of the haughty Duke of Burgundy. The calculating Burgundy duke was busy consolidating his alliance with the English king when suddenly on December 18, 1415, his son-in-law, the syphilitic Dauphin Louis, died, a victim of his own excesses. Next in line for the throne was John, Count of Touraine, the 15-year-old second son of King Charles VI and Isabel, who lived with his wife's family, staunch Burgundians. Then to compound matters, the old Duke of Berry died, leaving no heirs, and left the presiding seat of the King's Council vacant. Louis II of Anjou became President of the King's Council and was alarmed to see that after all the Royalist campaigns to protect the Valois throne the new dauphin, future King John, would simply step over to the Burgundian side. In haste the Duke of Anjou sent for young Charles to come to Paris and begin his political apprenticeship.

So, in June 1416, Charles, a sad and frightened 13 year old, accompanied by Marie, bade a tearful farewell to the companions of the only pleasant years of his childhood to return to the sinister atmosphere of a bankrupt and brutally cruel Paris. Once again he was surrounded by filth, starvation, death, plotters, murderers, and maniacs. To his horror he was reunited with his parents, who were greatly changed for the worse: King Charles VI was catatonic and Queen Isabel was morose, having grown obese to the extent that she could barely stand. The queen, still espousing all causes in the hope that she would be on the right side no matter what happened, suggested a reconciliation with her son John the new dauphin. But before the Duke of Burgundy could arrange the dauphin's triumphal entrance into Paris, planned for mid-April 1417, the dauphin died mysteriously. He was found by the roadside on April 5, probably poisoned, with "his body, tongue and lips extraordinarily swollen and his eyes bulging out of his head."

Thus Charles, at fourteen, became the dauphin of France. He was officially invested with the duchies of Dauphine, Touraine, and Berry; proclaimed heir to the Valois throne; and as dauphin of France took his place on the King's Council. Just weeks later catastrophe struck when he lost his brave protector and most sagacious advisor—the Duke of Anjou, who died suddenly in May after a brief illness. Bitterly mourned by Charles, Yolande, his family, and his subjects, Louis II left a huge void in their lives.

Charles, an adolescent in Paris, was surrounded by enemies; he was misshapen and awkward and still melancholy and mistrusting. Given these handicaps, he also understandably lacked confidence. The future looked abysmal.

CHAPTER FIVE

Yolande, now Dowager Duchess of Anjou, was very aware of the dangers whirling about Charles, and she acted in her usual clear-sighted and cool-headed way. She arranged for young Marie to live permanently with Charles in Paris so as not to cut him off from all his Anjou family at once, and she personally selected a solid guard of precepts, all loyal and reliable men, to advise him and cushion him from enemy plots. Thus Yolande could guide and protect Charles, even from a great distance. After all, her own Anjou interests were inextricably linked to the House of Valois.

But even Yolande could not shield the dauphin from his own scheming mother. Only days after the death of the Dauphin John, Isabel, who had apparently recovered from her shock in no time, insisted that Charles come to stay with her at the royal Chateau de Vincennes. There Charles found a human menagerie that only his mother could have assembled: her own numerous and unscrupulous lovers, among them Pierre de Giac, George de La Tremoille, Louis de Boisredon, and other captains and pages; dozens of the most vulgar ladies of the court and their own lovers; buffoons; musicians; astrologers; assorted hangers-on; and some members of the political fringe. Charles, in the midst of this round-the-clock orgy, must have longed to escape, but he could not have imagined the conditions under which he would soon leave Vincennes.

On April 15, just ten days after the death of the Dauphin John, poor King Charles VI, dressed up in a kingly fashion for service, rode toward Vincennes, this time accompanied by the ally of Armagnac and Provost of Paris, Tanguy du Chatel, and a small army of men. Alerted of the king's arrival, Queen Isabel sent the Dauphin Charles to greet him, escorted by Boisredon and a few soldiers. The two small and unlikely forces met halfway between the town and the chateau; within minutes Boisredon had been arrested in the king's name by du Chatel and the Armagnacs, and the young Charles was obliged to return to Paris with his babbling invalid father. The next day, after a brief court hearing, the condemned Boisredon was floating down the Seine, tied up in a leather bag on which was written "Make way for the King's justice."

Two days later Queen Isabel was forced into exile by Tanguy du Chatel and sent to her chateau in Tours in the company of her daughter Catherine, the future Queen of England. All of her own dozen or so houses and chateaux were confiscated and pillaged of their treasures, collected over 25 years by the greedy queen. Most of the valuables went to the instigator Armagnac, but he had many ready partners with whom to share the spoils. This was all done officially in the name of the king, the poor lunatic puppet king, who was brought out of confinement whenever it suited whoever wanted to use him, then returned to his madness alone.

The frenzied queen, stripped of her outrageous court, her menagerie of monkeys and birds, and her retinue of servants, was kept under house arrest by unsympathetic Armagnac guards. Filled with a venomous hatred for the new Dauphin Charles, she blamed him for everything.

Poor Charles was the last person to bear responsibility. Although he was quite old enough at fourteen to understand his duties, he was far too young and inexperienced to carry them out. Timid and unsure of himself, he was the pawn of his many advisors, most of whom were initially protectors of the House of Valois and allies of the Count of Armagnac. By now the Count of Armagnac had become too strong and independent for the good of the crown and had lost touch with the cause he had originally started out to serve.

Yolande d'Anjou, worried that Armagnac's influence would eventually harm the Royalist cause, stepped in once again to help her son-in-law. Under the pretext of wanting him to tour the southern provinces, she brought Charles back to the Loire and he was only too happy to return. During the month of June 1417, accompanied by Yolande and Marie and some of his other Anjou cousins, the dauphin travelled from city to city, from province to province, meeting with the local landlords and making public speeches. Yolande, herself titular queen of four kingdoms (Sicily, Cyprus, Jerusalem, and Naples) was teaching him in her subtle yet persistent way to develop confidence and behave like a king. He enjoyed the tours, gained a little assurance, and spoke well in public in a deep voice that was pleasant to the ear, one of his few appealing physical qualities. He was extremely polite to everyone, even pretending not to hear the derision behind his back, the cruel references to himself as the bastard son of the German queen and the Duke of Orléans. Yolande heard the remarks, however, and from then on everyone was instructed to refer to Charles not only as the dauphin but as the only son of the king of France and sole heir to the French crown. During his month-long tour he gained many new adherents to the Royalist cause from servants to noblemen. Perhaps through association with this successful tour he developed a taste for the nomadic existence he would lead for the rest of his life.

His triumphant tour of the southern provinces completed, Charles was now to play another princely role, this one on the battlefield. The port city of Rouen in Normandy had fallen, taken by the Burgundian forces, and Yolande d'Anjou decided it should be the duty of the dauphin to bring Rouen back into the Royal sphere. Wearing his first suit of armor, newly made especially for him with deeply sloping shoulders and the fleur de lys emblem on his long and narrow chest, he was probably unaware of his comical appearance as he rode proudly to battle at the end of July 1417.

He adapted readily to army camp life, and the fourteen-year-old prince won the respect and even affection of his soldiers through his gentle manners and modest bearing. Charles ate the same food as his army and, like them, slept on a bed of straw. Never to be a great soldier, the Valois prince was an able one, and victory at Rouen was quick for the Royalists. Its fruits were to be short-lasting, though: The English had once again landed on the Normandy coast.

King Henry V and his mighty army disembarked at Trouville in the middle of August 1417. By August 20, Caen had already capitulated to the English. King Henry V then divided his army into equal groups that fanned out in three directions in his aim to take all of Normandy. Bayeux fell and then Argentan and Alençon and other towns in rapid succession; the local garrisons of Royalist soldiers were executed and the Norman population was given the choice of becoming English or leaving Normandy altogether. Many opted to remain and become subjects of King Henry. Those who fled left their belongings behind. The victorious English troops then marched to Rouen, the Royalist Norman capital determined to resist capture, and laid a siege that would last a year.

The Duke of Burgundy met personally with the jubilant English king in October 1417, when they spent a festive week together, culminating with Burgundy's formal pledge of allegiance to Henry V. For the first time and from then on the Burgundians officially acknowledged the English king as the rightful heir to the throne in France.

The dauphin, meanwhile, had returned to Paris, to the once-raucous Petit-Musc of his childhood, now somber and filled with ghosts from the past. What terror he must have felt when he learned that the Duke of Burgundy's army of forty-thousand men was marching toward Paris! The Duke himself had published a manifesto declaring King Charles VI mentally unfit to rule and the dauphin, at fifteen, too young. With that he negated the Valois right to rule and heralded the new King Henry V of England and France.

In fact, Charles had neither the intellect nor the imagination to react to the political situation and was singularly incapable of deciding France's future. He was completely dependent on others for help and advice and lacked both the charisma and the stamina to enter into any independent thought or action. His cousin Burgundy was the most powerful political figure in Paris; helpless, all that the Dauphin Charles could do was to wait at Petit-Musc for news from the outside. After all, he was only fifteen.

Still, in Paris he must have been appalled to learn early in May 1418 that his mother had been freed from house arrest. In a dramatic escape arranged by Burgundy's men, Queen Isabel had evaded her Armagnac captors all the way from Tours to Paris. Accompanied by the Duke of Burgundy, the queen made a triumphant entry into the city, where she reclaimed her old title of regent.

On the night of May 28, 1418 the Burgundian troops entered Paris unexpectedly and took over the strategic points throughout the city after little combat. The following morning the Duke of Burgundy paid a visit to the lunatic King Charles VI, who greeted him by saying, "Dear cousin, how can I thank you for your many kindnesses to the Queen?" The traitor duke controlled the king, the queen, and all of Paris. But his intentions were to rule all of France on behalf of the King of England, and to that end he needed to have the dauphin under his aegis—or do away with him altogether.

Had Charles not been guided by his "bonne mère" Yolande d'Anjou he might easily have been swayed by the strength of Burgundy and his allies. Charles had a weak character, and cordial relations with the Duke of Burgundy could have made the dauphin's immediate life more agreeable. Fortunately the young Valois prince had grasped the importance of his responsibility to safeguard his father's throne and bravely would not even meet with the Duke of Burgundy.

A week after Paris had been taken by the Burgundians the Count of Armagnac was able to persuade Charles that between his own Gascon army and the dauphin's Royalist troops, they could overthrow the Duke of Burgundy. Their attempt was a dismal failure; the Parisians spontaneously showed a rousing support for the forces of the invincible Duke. Seeing that there was no hope of victory, Armagnac's beaten soldiers retreated from Paris and now the dauphin's very life was in danger. Rescued from the Petit-Musc in the middle of the night by Tanguy du Chatel, the wily Provost of Paris and Armagnac supporter, Charles had no choice but to flee Paris, bitter and broken; it would be nineteen years before he would return to the city he had come to hate.

For once Charles did not return to the Loire Valley. Tanguy du Chatel was anxious to replace Yolande of Anjou as Charles's principal advisor and the dauphin, at fifteen, needed an experienced statesman to guide him. Together they went to Bourges, the ancient capital of Gaul, in the center of France. Du Chatel had been a chamberlain of the Duke d'Orléans, and after the murder of Orléans, du Chatel became closely associated with the Armagnacs. His long friendship with Louis d'Anjou and his deep hatred for the Burgundians made him a man Charles could trust. Tanguy du Chatel was middle-aged, about fifty, by the time he became Charles's new mentor, and with his many years of political mastery he was just the right man at the right time. The young dauphin respected du Chatel, and under the provost's clever tutelage gained some political maturity.

September 1418 brought a blood bath to Paris. Tens of thousands of innocent people, including the elderly and women and children, were slaughtered by bloodthirsty fighters from all factions. They roamed the streets day and night, their butchery unchecked and unpunished. These massacres stopped only because of an epidemic of the plague and the subsequent vast piles of rotting bodies all over the city. The plague claimed a further 50,000 lives during the winter. In Bourges the dauphin was horrified by the daily reports from Paris; feeling frustrated and inept, he was unable to take a decision to act.

About this time Charles learned that Tours, a Royalist city on the Loire, was in the hands of a large Burgundian army. He took an unusual step, probably born of the frustration of helplessness: Hastily he gathered a small army and rode out to quell the rebellion. It was not characteristic of him to proceed spontaneously, and his small army had not been well-prepared for battle. They were made to beat a nearly immediate retreat in the face of the Duke of Burgundy's superior fighting force.

On his return to Bourges, slouched at the head of his defeated troops, he passed next to a garrison of Burgundian soldiers at Azay-le-Rideau. One of the enemy soldiers recognized the dauphin and called aloud that Charles was the bastard son of a whore. Battered and humiliated, Charles, who was neither violent nor cruel, gave the command and in just a few short hours, by the end of the afternoon, the entire Burgundian garrison had been massacred. It would be Charles's first and last cruel act.

Toward the end of autumn 1418, more and more newly loyal Frenchmen, having had enough of war and civil strife throughout the country, made their way to Bourges to promise fidelity to the dauphin. Encouraged by this burst of allegiance, Charles proclaimed himself regent on October 26th and established his own government with Bourges as its capital. Now France had two regents, two Parliaments, two councils, and two monies of equal value.

The French had as options an obese, middle-aged, Bavarian nymphomaniac regent, mentally unstable and controlled by the Duke of Burgundy, and her son, the dauphin. It should have been an obvious choice, but the queen was allied to the English king, who was powerful, and the Duke of Burgundy, who was rich, and poor Charles was yet uninspiring.

At the time the dauphin–regent was nearly sixteen; he was ugly, ungainly, and sadly lacked in brilliance and charm. Stiff, insular, and vague, he still depended on others for counsel, which he did not always heed. Charles was, however, basically intelligent, polite and patient, and extremely pious. He was not a coward. It was his great instability that worried people, his lifelong romance with astrology, and his wanderlust. Ever restless, the dauphin could not stay long in one place, moving from chateau to chateau every few days, mindless of the confusion it caused others. He was egotistical and dreamy and dour and already was more attracted by the company of scoundrels than of good men. He combined low morals with deep piety to an unusual degree, reflecting the whole spectrum of role models he had had since birth. That is not in itself shocking in an adolescent, but Charles, having had to grow up prematurely, remained in many ways mentally and spiritually stunted until the end of his life.

Yolande of Anjou, who had made her decision long ago to guide, teach, and defend Charles, had other important missions as the energetic Dowager Queen of Sicily that obligated her to make long and arduous journeys, criss-crossing France and the Italian Mediterranean coast. While she was away she sent the Count of Richemont to keep an eye on the dauphin and report to her his comings and goings.

Arthur de Richemont was only ten years older than the dauphin. The second son of the independent Duke of Britanny, his sympathies were with the English, but before long he was won over to the Valois cause by Tanguy du Chatel. His widowed mother had married King Henry IV of England, but Arthur had fought on the French side, had been wounded at the battle of Agincourt, and was taken prisoner by the English. Freed on ransom Richemont became an active and loyal supporter of the Royalist cause and eventually replaced Tanguy du Chatel as the uncompromising and protective tutor of the Dauphin Charles.

When she was in France, Charles's "bonne mère" spent as much time with Charles as he would allow, his new independence having gone somewhat to his head. Yolande recognized, as Agnès Sorel would twenty years later, that Charles was not incapable but simply lacking in confidence and discipline, undoubtedly suffering from early psychological wounds that had etched themselves permanently into his character.

Having taught the dauphin how to behave like a king, Yolande now did everything possible to convince him of the nearly sacred importance of his mission. She cleverly cajoled King Charles VI into signing a royal decree naming Charles lieutenant general of the kingdom, a title that increased the authority of the hesitant Charles and gave further credibility to his legitimacy.

Queen Isabel, fretting in Paris, decided it was high time that she reclaim her son, using every ruse she could imagine. She sent Charles gifts, letters, and ambassadors with messages of maternal concern and affection, but the wise Aragon princess once aware of this sudden maternal interest, was not to be taken in. It was too obvious that the foolish mother only wanted to use the boy to further her own devious interests and that she would ultimately deliver the dauphin to the Duke of Burgundy. Not mincing her words, Yolande wrote to Isabel: "A woman given so many lovers has no need for a child. Having neither nourished him nor raised him until now, you would let him die like his brothers, become English like yourself, or drive him mad like his father. I will keep him. Come and take him if you dare." Charles remained in the Loire Valley under the watchful eye of Yolande.

CHAPTER SIX

The English siege of Rouen had not let up. The heroic Rouennais were starving, and their determined leader, Alain Blanchard, was forced to reduce their numbers. Ten thousand hapless people were sent out of the embattled city; not allowed to cross the English lines surrounding Rouen, they had perished from hunger, cold, sickness, and fatigue. The dauphin could do nothing to help the city, and his army risked certain defeat at the hands of the well-prepared English.

Rouen capitulated and King Henry V entered the city on January 19, 1419. Alain Blanchard and those Rouennais who refused to recognize English sovereignty were decapitated, but otherwise the city was taken without pillage or punishment. In less than 18 months Henry V had taken all of Normandy, with the exception of Mont Saint-Michel. More confident than ever, he minted coins inscribed "Henricus Rex Franciae" and began preparations to march on Paris.

The Duke of Burgundy, by now long accustomed to the role of master of the kingdom, was distressed to realize that Henry V would no longer need his Burgundian allies. The English king had made great military strides without Burgundian forces, and now Henry V made it clear that he would rule France alone. John of Burgundy had never considered losing his own power, and he was as intolerant of opposition as was the ruthless Henry. The Duke of Burgundy re-examined his relationship with the English king and concluded that perhaps the dauphin could still be useful.

Double-faced and power hungry, the Duke of Burgundy was in a desperate situation. Anxious to strengthen his own position by any pretense, he sent an urgent message to Charles that he had reconsidered his alliance with the King of England and was prepared to join forces with the dauphin to drive the English out of France.

There is no record of Charles's immediate reaction to his cousin's offer; one may assume that it was at the least a guarded one. Nevertheless, the two men, each accompanied by a small army, met at Pouilly on July 8, 1419. The Duke of Burgundy bent one knee in calculated homage to the gangling youth before him. After three days of discussion, during which the Duke of Burgundy coolly denied having ever wanted to encourage his English alliance, they agreed to sign a preliminary pact of friendship and to meet again in September in Montereau on the banks of the River Yonne, just where it flows into the Seine.

On Sunday, September 10, the two princes faced each other across the river. The chateau de Montereau had been given over to the Duke of Burgundy; the dauphin lived in an encampment on the opposite bank. The Duke of Burgundy, long called John the Fearless by his people, had attended an early mass that morning and was unusually agitated by a feeling of foreboding that his life was in peril. Charles had heard from his own men of a possible attempt on his life and he, too, felt the ominous presentiment of danger. No one had forgotten the murder of the Duke of Orléans.

Their meeting, which was to be held in a small wooden pavilion in the middle of the Montereau bridge especially constructed by Tanguy du Chatel for this event, was delayed two hours, during which the two mutually mistrusting principals sent flurries of messages across the river Yonne. Finally, at five o'clock, the cousins, each escorted by the ten chevaliers to which they were limited by agreement, made their solemn way toward the pavilion on the bridge. As at Pouilly, the Duke kneeled before Charles, calling him "my honored lord," and no sooner had the dauphin ordered him to rise than John the Fearless began to recite his long list of denials, promises, and sugar-coated lies to the suspicious 16 year old. When the dauphin replied with thinly veiled accusations aimed at the duke, one of Burgundy's men became nervous and half drew his sword. Within seconds all swords were drawn and clanking, but Tanguy du Chatel caught hold of the dauphin and whisked him off the bridge to safety. Minutes later, John the Fearless was dead, killed in the confusion by an unknown hand, his skull split with an axe. The opening of his cranium was to be called "the hole through which the English entered France."

The dauphin, an unwitting accomplice to the assassination, was nevertheless immediately presumed guilty of the murder and was forced to bear the heavy responsibility for a crime that he, it is fairly certain, did not commit. Fleeing to the Loire Valley as he usually did in times of trouble, he wrote hundreds of letters and circulars protesting his innocence. They were in vain.

Queen Isabel sent long hysterical missives to the pope and to most of the crowned heads of Europe accusing her son of murder. With Isabel's help, even the witless Charles VI published a letter in which the foolish king accuses his own son of "patricide, criminal *lese-majesty,* destruction of the common cause, being the enemy of God and justice" and entreats the people to disavow their dauphin–regent.

Many points remain unclear regarding the murky conspiracy to assassinate the Duke of Burgundy. In some circles it was said that Burgundy himself had intended to murder Charles and Tanguy du Chatel had learned of the plot and preempted his enemy. Then there were the Armagnacs, still eager to avenge the death of Louis of Orléans; they had every reason to wish to see Burgundy dead. It was even hinted that Yolande d'Araon, the Dowager Queen of Sicily, had ordered the Duke of Burgundy's assassination to advance her son-in-law's cause. In any case, the harm was done and Charles was presumed guilty.

The many political factions in France were rife with spies, double agents, and informers. The hapless Charles was forced to lie low in the Loire Valley, still protesting his innocence but largely cut off from the rest of France. No one knew what would happen next. Would the King of England march on Paris? Could someone be plotting Charles's imminent death? Uncertainty reigned. Had Charles intended the murder of the Duke of Burgundy, he might have been prepared to take advantage of the chaos that would follow. It is a sign of his innocence that all he could do was cower in his beloved Loire Valley while the Parisians mourned the once powerful Burgundian. The duke's funeral mass at Notre Dame was the most splendid ever held in France. According to the chronicles, the "Bourgeois of Paris" (who was a staunch Burgundian) published that the 50,000 candles and torches cost three thousand pounds, and the entire cathedral was hung with black cloth and decorated with the arms of the House of Burgundy. Thousands attended to hear the pious sermon given by the rector of the University of Paris and to pay their last respects to John the Fearless. Buried in the magnificent Burgundian mausoleum near Dijon, his tomb is grander than that of any French king.

The successor to the Burgundy dukedom, John's son Philip was a highly intelligent and chivalrous young man, not naturally given to politics or intrigue. Married to Charles's older sister Michelle, Duke Philip hesitated before he renewed his father's allegiance to Henry V. Later to be called Philip the Wise or Philip the Good, the pragmatic new Duke of Burgundy did not hasten into any act of vengeance and, it is probable that he himself believed his brother-in-law the dauphin–regent to be innocent of the plot to assassinate his father. But the Burgundian troops and the Parisians were all in favor of the English alliance; the dauphin–regent's star had suddenly dipped over the horizon. Duke Philip of Burgundy had a monster of a mother-in-law in Queen Isabel; he had no choice but to proffer his liege to Henry V.

Meeting in early December 1419 at Arras, halfway between Paris and Calais, the new Duke of Burgundy and Henry V signed the preliminary agreements to the treaty of Troyes, which would eventually remove the last obstacles blocking Henry's quest for the French throne. The definitive treaty was signed in Troyes on May 20, 1420 and was proclaimed in the cathedral of Troyes the following day in the presence of Henry V; Charles VI and the wicked Isabel; Duke Philip, called the Good, of Burgundy and his duchess; and most of the royal family and their courts. The dauphin, of course, was absent. His incoherent father, dressed up as king and enthroned on a dais covered with golden fleur de lys, must have enjoyed the splendid pageantry organized for the occasion as he listened, understanding nothing, to the thirty-three articles of the treaty, supposedly drawn up by his own hand. Read aloud before the sumptuously dressed audience, the treaty began, "Charles, by the Grace of God, King of France, salutes you. In the interest of permanent peace a final agreement was drawn up and signed today in the city of Troyes by us and our very dear and beloved son Henry V, King of England and heir and Regent of France, in our name." The chief clauses of the treaty gave Princess Catherine's hand in marriage to King Henry V and to their descendants the perpetual right to rule the two countries as one. The treaty stipulated that King Charles VI and Queen Isabel would keep all their titles, rights, and properties until their deaths but that Henry would nonetheless govern the country alone as he saw fit, as dauphin and regent, becoming king upon Charles VI's eventual death. Finally it stated that Charles Valois, the "supposed Dauphin" and "so-called son of the king," should thereafter be considered an imposter, a murderer, and a usurper of the throne. The treaty specifically put his legitimacy in doubt and retracted all his rights. The mental deficiency of Charles VI should not be underestimated. He was completely mad and did not have the capacity to grasp the meaning of the proclamation; he was probably not able to understand even that he had a son. He was simply the pitiful pawn of his perfidious queen and of the formidable alliance, never stronger than now, of the English king and the Duke of Burgundy.

Married to Catherine of France two festive weeks later in the cathedral of Troyes, King Henry immediately left his bride to enjoy her new exalted role as Queen of England and future Queen of France. His first actions as the son-in-law of the King of France were to lay siege to Montereau and Melun and take the towns in the name of their king. His short campaign over, Henry V and his queen made their magnificent royal entrance into Paris on the first day of December 1420 accompanied by King Charles VI, Queen Isabel, and the Duke and Duchess of Burgundy. The Estates General and the University of

Paris formally received King Henry V as Regent of France on December 6 and unanimously approved the Treaty of Troyes, pledging their fidelity to both kings and to the future united kingdom of England and France.

As regent King Henry V had every intention to continue his campaign against Charles the Dauphin, the other regent. Not willing to further tax his grumbling English subjects, he ordered a new stricter program of taxation in Paris, a heavy load for the poor and already overtaxed population. Threatened with prison, no one dared to object to these new taxes; thus one eighth of all the money in circulation in Paris was collected by the English king toward his effort to overthrow the French king's son.

Encouraged by his reception in the French capital, Henry gave a series of fêtes at his residence in the Louvre during the Christmas holidays. Then, partly to please the Dowager Duchess of Burgundy, widow of John the Fearless, on January 3, Henry V went a step further: He declared the dauphin Charles guilty of murder, disinherited, and banished from the kingdom forever.

Henry V then prepared to return to England after an absence of three years. His war in France was proving longer and costlier than the English Parliament was prepared to pay for, greedy relatives had their eyes on his throne, and the people were beginning to complain that their king had deserted them. Accompanied by Queen Catherine, King Henry left France under the care of his brother the Duke of Clarence.

CHAPTER SEVEN

Charles, despondent but safe in the Loire, turned to Yolande for advice. Bitterly disappointed by the recent events in the north, she nevertheless encouraged Charles to move, to travel to make himself known as the dauphin in the central and southern regions of France, which were outside of Burgundian influence. During his previous visits to the provinces, he had become acquainted with many of the noble families in Lyon, Nîmes, and Poitiers and once again they received him with enthusiasm, particularly the provincial youth, and promised him their allegiance. His confidence growing and his army newly enforced with young recruits loyal to the Valois cause, in February 1421, Charles was given further reason to rejoice: John Stuart, the Scottish Earl of Buchan, landed at La Rochelle with six thousand men. The Scotts had their own long quarrels with the English king and were more than ready to help the French prince.

Charles, with spirits mounting and anxious to encourage the morale of his supporters, dreamed of a dramatic victory on the battlefield. But where? King Henry's brother, the Duke of Clarence, provided the answer. Clarence had been forbidden by the English king to fight on enemy territory; English military strategy was based on laying long siege rather than on lightning attacks or pitched battle. The Duke of Clarence, however, attempted several forays into the Loire region and at first met with easy success. Purposely misinformed by spies that the dauphin's Scottish mercenaries were near Angers and unprepared to fight, Clarence (remembering Azincourt) couldn't resist the sure victory that would be his. In mid-March 1421, the Duke of Clarence led a small English army, without its excellent archers, into attack at Baugé on a waiting and well-prepared Franco-Scottish army of some 5,000, including 1,000 archers. Clarence was among the first to be killed, followed into death by two hundred English soldiers. By the time the Earl of Salisbury and his troops could come to their rescue, the English had suffered a resounding defeat.

In Poitiers awaiting news of the battle, Charles was elated by the victory—it was the first time the English had been defeated on a French battlefield during his lifetime. The battle of Baugé was not Azincourt, nor was it a turning point in French history; but it was the shot in the arm that the Royalist forces needed to become optimistic for the future of the realm. The Dauphin Charles became more actively interested in organizing his forces and more confident in his ability to do so. Alas, his confidence was but a very thin veneer, easily shattered and never long-lasting, soon to be shattered again.

King Henry V, in England raising funds for his French campaign, was outraged by the English losses at Baugé. Convinced that he had divine approval to rule France and that God was on his side, the English defeat at Baugé unsettled Henry. At last relatively solvent, he gathered a force of about twenty thousand men, including 3,500 archers, and in June 1421 set sail from Dover to Calais, anxious to conquer once and for all the realm he was determined to call his own. Splitting his army into three divisions, which successfully took several important towns and cities west and south of Paris, Henry then reunited his forces at Meaux, a dauphinist stronghold. There was no sign of the dauphin, who had retreated south of the Loire, unwilling to match his meager troops against the English. Throughout the autumn and winter Henry laid siege to the fortress-like city, personally supervising his troops. Meaux finally fell in early spring. King Henry was master of an ever-growing portion of France; fully one quarter of the country was under Lancastrian authority—Normandy in the northwest, Guyenne in the southwest and the north-central part of France, the Ile de France including Paris, from the Somme to the Loire.

Now, at the close of 1421 he had another reason to consolidate his rule on France: In Paris on December 6, 1421, Queen Catherine gave birth to a boy, the future Henry VI. Thousands of church bells pealed joyously over the French capital as heralds proclaimed, "The Dauphin is born!" Prayers were offered at Notre Dame for the baby prince, and free bread and wine were distributed in the streets of Paris. But no amount of celebration could erase what no one yet knew, which was that the newborn prince Henry had inherited the madness of his Valois grandfather Charles VI.

Henry V was powerful, but the English had become increasingly unpopular with the bourgeois and the masses, and by 1422 it had at least become clear to the French that it was not in their interests to have a foreign ruler. Lancastrian France was over-ridden with English soldiers who, underpaid and far from home, continued to rape and ransack the French countryside. French agriculture was at a standstill without crops or livestock; villages and entire fields lay blackened and empty as thousands of Frenchmen fled the brutal English presence.

Henry V was impervious to the sufferings of the rural French and as fervent as ever in his conviction that his was a divine duty to punish the French for their sins. Brilliant warrior that he was, he now determined to engage the Dauphin Charles and the Royalists forces in battle. Leading his army on a march toward the Loire to join waiting Burgundian troops, Henry V was forced by illness to stop at Corbeil, only fifteen miles south of Paris. In spite of his lifelong great physical strength, formidable discipline, and ferocious will power, the English king had suffered from flagging health since the long siege at Meaux, and now at the last minute he was forced to abandon his attack on the dauphin's army. After two weeks at Corbeil, no longer strong enough to mount his own horse, Henry was carried by litter to his favorite chateau at Vincennes, where he was met by his brother John, Duke of Bedford. (It is interesting to note that he did not ask to see Catherine, his queen, who was a mere three miles away in Paris.)

Aware that his end was near, the English king gave his brother the Duke of Bedford the responsibility of governing France as regent and to his brother the Duke of Gloucester the protectorate of England, with the stipulation that both would recognize and defend the nine-month-old Henry as heir to the two thrones.

Warrior until the end, his dying regret was that he would not be able to liberate Jerusalem from the Turks. Suffering from complications of dysentery and fever and agonizing with pain, Henry V died on August 31, 1422. He was only thirty-five years old.

His flesh was then boiled off his bones, one of the royal rites of death during the medieval age, and the skeleton of Henry V was dressed in leather and blessed at the first funeral mass at the Basilica of St. Denis. Two months later the King of England and would-be King of France was buried in Westminster Abbey.

Seven weeks after Henry's sudden death, the king who had never really been king died in Paris. Charles VI, French history's most tragic monarch, had lived the past twenty-nine years in the foggy world of the hopelessly insane. During his long reign he had sired eleven royal children, seen civil war and famine engulf his country, disinherited his only surviving son, and signed away his throne to an ancient foe. Protected in a way by his madness he died almost alone, as he had lived, in the Hotel Saint-Paul, on October 21 1422 at the age of fifty-four. The faithful Odette de Champsdivers and his priest were by the king's side, but no one in the family came to his funeral, not even Isabel or the Duke of Burgundy; the Duke of Bedford was the sole royal attendant. Curiously, the crowds that lined the streets on the outskirts of Paris wept openly as his coffin was carried to the Basilica of Saint Denis, the final resting place of all French kings. He had been their king for forty-two years and, sane or insane, they held an affection for him and their king was dead. But when they shouted, "The King is dead, long live the King!" in the streets of Paris, they were wishing long life to the baby King Henry VI who lived across the Channel.

The true French heir was in Bourges, unable to make the decision to claim the throne without first hearing what his Council of State and specifically Yolande of Aragon had to say. Encouraged by everyone around him he declared himself king and, prodded by Yolande, who had travelled to Bourges to be present for the coronation, Charles, nervous and hesitant, was pronounced King Charles VII of France on October 30, 1422. It was not the traditional sacrament of a French king; that sacrament would take place many years later in Reims in the presence of Joan of Arc. But for many countrymen the solemn and majestic ceremony in the small cathedral of Bourges meant hope for the future of France.

For the time being, Charles VII was only effectively the king of Bourges, the seat of his government, and the people in Paris referred to him mockingly as the Kinglet of Bourges. His status had, nonetheless, changed, and from the day he was pronounced king, Charles VII was always treated as a royal.

Now everyone was deferential toward him, standing as he left or entered a room, inclining their heads when he passed, kneeling in his presence. Nomad that he was, he continued to move from chateau to chateau, but now the whole country would turn out to greet him and bid him farewell. A deeply pious man, his first act upon entering a town was to visit the church or monastery. On those days the refectory tables were set with special china and the king was served the finest wines by the monks who felt honored by the royal presence. Not to put the piety of Charles VII in doubt, the truth was that he probably had better food when he dined with the monks; the king himself was very poor. At his own miserable court Charles couldn't even pay for a sole, not even on feast days. A mocking little song of the day describes the simple fare at Charles's table:

Un jour que LaHire et Poton	*One day LaHire and Poton*
Le vinrent voir par festoiement,	*Came to feast with the king,*
N'avaient qu'une queue de mouton	*And there was a sheep's tail*
Et deux poulets tant seulement.	*And two chickens only.*

The new king's military forces were as meager as his meals. In all, he had about forty lancers of his own and a few horses; Charles himself often travelled on mule-back. Eventually several thousand Gascons came to Bourges to join the others loyal to France but they, too, were without money. The Gascons were followed by hundreds of Breton soldiers, who took up Charles's banner out of their own deep hatred for the English. Lombard mercenaries began to arrive, a few at a time, until they were nearly as strong a force as the Scots. When the king couldn't pay for their services in Ecus, which was most often the case, he paid them in land. The domains of King Charles VII were in the mildest region of France with the richest earth, beautiful rivers abounding in fish, great oak forests with animals for hunting, fields of wheat, and countless vineyards and fruit orchards. He actually controlled most of France south of the region surrounding the Loire, including Lyon in the east, to the port— the only Royalist port on the western coast of France—of La Rochelle on the Atlantic. But he didn't have enough to do; without money and without strong allies he could not face the enemy in pitched battle. He was solitary and nomadic, melancholy and indecisive; Charles's face reflected the sadness and humiliation of his youth and the uncertainty of his future. At one time during 1423, he considered escape from all responsibility, leaving France to the tenacious English to live in permanent exile in Spain or Scotland. It was probably his listlessness or infernal indecision that prevented him from flight rather than a positive determination to stay and fight for his country. His preoccupation—it bordered on obsession—with astrology was well-known and he saw astrologers daily. They might have given him hope for the future, which would have encouraged him to remain in France. In any case, he remained.

Married to saintly Marie d'Anjou, in August 1422, in the small cathedral of Bourges, Charles might have felt he was marrying his sister. Not that his life-long platonic love for Marie hindered in any way his conjugal duties: The queen gave birth to fourteen children over the next twenty-three years!

But their life at court, mainly in Bourges, was far from Jolly. The king and queen ate at separate tables, served by their private attendants, in an atmosphere more like that of a convent than a royal court. Queen Marie was far from being pretty, having, a contemporary wrote, "a face that would frighten even the English," but she was the sweetest and simplest of women and blindly devoted to her husband throughout her life with "the passionate love of a blushing bride." As sedentary as the king was nomadic, Marie spent her days praying, embroidering, and fretting over her frail children, surrounded by her dull and pious ladies-in-waiting, very much in the tradition of the French queens up until the odious Isabel.

The king's needs were few: He ate and drank very little and spent most of his time in one room brooding, wherever he was. In the mornings he attended three masses, one after another, and hunted during the afternoons. In between these activities he habitually shunned company and stayed locked up in his apartments. This was unusual behavior in the fifteenth century because real privacy did not exist at the time; private life was rather the concept of a group or a family doing something together. For most people there simply wasn't room to be alone, and for royals it wasn't the custom. During the evenings he conferred with his astrologers or met with an advisor, such as Tanguy du Chatel or Arthur de Richemont. Sometimes he played chess or backgammon or tried his luck at card games, which had recently been introduced into France from Italy and were in the form of Tarot cards. But destiny, after all, plays the greatest role in people's lives, and it was about this time that Agnès Sorel was born. Charles's life can be roughly divided into two segments: before Agnès and after Agnès. He was suspicious and superstitious and never crossed a bridge if he could avoid it, remembering Montereau. On feast days he would invite a bishop or an abbey to his table but was uncomfortable to have anyone in his presence who was not already known to him.

It must have rankled Charles, inert and silent in Bourges, to hear that the Duke of Bedford had set up a well-organized administration in France in the name of his tiny nephew across the Channel, while he, Charles, the rightful King of France, had barely a glimmer of hope for the future of his own baby son, the future Louis XI, who was born in Bourges on July 3, 1423. His despair was bred in his sense of helplessness, and his helplessness was a result of his despair. So he did nothing.

CHAPTER EIGHT

The Duke of Bedford was a brilliant administrator, reorganizing the Guilds and Corporations of the Halles and giving them considerable privileges; he further increased his popularity by offering the bourgeoisie loans to help them rebuild their ruined houses. He imposed rent control and divided Paris into several "arrondissements," each with its own magistrate, and generally restored some measure of order to the most violent of cities, where packs of wolves roamed the streets at night.

In Paris, Normandy, and the other provinces under English control he allowed the French to govern themselves with a large majority of French members in every city and municipal council while keeping a close eye on the clergy. His secret police were widespread and well-informed and his judicial arm was rigorous, to say the least. Ironically, the flaw in Bedford's regency was the English army. Although relatively few in number (he could call for thousands of reinforcements from across the Channel at short notice) and well-disciplined in battle, they wrought disaster on the local towns and countryside whenever they left the confines of their fortresses and garrisons.

Bedford was a well-organized regent. Three hundred English soldiers guarded the rights of little Henry VI in Paris—three hundred only in the now depopulated capital of about 100,000 Parisians. Those Frenchmen who hadn't lost their lives during the plague or run away from the political strife seemed relieved by the status quo; the Parisians were war-weary and happy to get on with their lives. One king or another made little difference in their daily existence; taxes were high and commerce reduced, but the bloodbath was over. The Duke of Bedford established his headquarters and residence in the Hotel des Tournelles, a stone's throw away from the Hotel Saint Paul, where the aging Queen Isabel lived. There Bedford lived in royal splendor, leaving England under the care of his uncle, Cardinal Henry, the Duke of Beaufort, and his brother Humphrey, the Duke of Gloucester.

Gloucester was an ambitious man, and England was a small country. Scanning the horizons for a not-too-distant province he could call his own, Duke Humphrey set his sights on the rich port city of Antwerp, the Hainault province, Holland, and Brabant. These rich lowland provinces were part and parcel of the Duke of Burgundy's principality, so his wrath knew no limits when Burgundy heard that Gloucester had disembarked at Calais in October 1424 with an army intending to march on Antwerp. Bedford dissuaded his brother at the last minute, and Gloucester and his army returned to England, but Philip the Good had learned his lesson and bent his course toward absolute autonomy from the English. He remained in his own territories and did not return to Paris for five years, until 1429.

The Treaty of Troyes was a legal document, but it could not remain a binding one. The fact that King Charles VI, who was insane, had been coerced into naming the English king heir to the French throne made the treaty wrong. The people realized this, and the Orléans–Armagnac alliance was a resistance movement and a play for power. But Charles of Orléans was still captive in England with his brother and thousands of French soldiers, and his release seemed doubtful. Count Bernard of Armagnac and his rowdy followers were behaving badly as the English soldiers raped, looted, and burned whenever they met with dissidents or poor people without anything to give to their cause.

While the Armagnacs terrorized the English-held countryside during the 1420s, Charles was at the same time unable to control them and was dependent on them for money and support.

There was nonetheless some activity at the court of the "Kinglet of Bourges." Charles VII had faithful friends in his cousin the Duke of Bourbon and his brother-in-law the young Duke of Anjou. Numerous other officers had left the Anglo-Burgundian alliance and had come to the Loire eager to serve their king.

Foreign mercenaries arrived from Italy, Switzerland, Germany, Scotland, and Spain to offer their services and hoped for battle. By 1425 the King of France had an army of thousands of men with nothing to do.

Gradually, though, the pattern of his life began to change. The petulant adolescent in Charles became increasingly bored with his lonely routine and he wanted some friends and distractions; he was in his mid-twenties and he was a husband, a father, and a king, but he'd thus far lived the life of a canon. Weak-minded and lacking good judgment, he became easy prey for the evil and ambitious, and, unfortunately, they were just the sort of people to whom he was attracted. Most of his new friends and advisors were of dubious character to say the least: Louvet, his cunning chief financier, offered his own daughters for the king's pleasure.

His mother-in-law still held some influence over Charles, but her many duties claimed most of her time and she could see him only occasionally. Each time she returned from a mission abroad Yolande did her best to counsel Charles and encourage him, and for a while after her visits he seemed inclined to follow her sage advice. But his bad habits and vice-ridden entourage triumphed over his weak resolve and he unfailingly fell back into the moral depths of his new associations. After having spent days alone, morose and apathetic, the king would join his raucous friends in a month-long frenzy of gambling, drinking, and womanizing, and he spent frequent and longer periods away from his family, most often at his chateau in Chinon. Whether in an insular or rambunctious mood, Charles never behaved like a king who was living on the edge of an abyss and never made any move to indicate that he was coping with problems of state. The people were beginning to say that Charles had inherited his father's mental frailty.

CHAPTER NINE

By the spring of 1425, conditions at the French court were unchanged. Despite the tireless efforts of Yolande d'Anjou, King Charles remained aloof and despondent. His wife, Queen Marie, had given birth to two children. Steadfast, pious, and loyal, Marie spent most of her time at the Chateau of Mehun-sur-Yvres, near Bourges, devoted to her husband and family. Although strong enough to withstand the vicissitudes of her life as queen, Marie was not charismatic enough to hold any influence whatsoever over her moody husband.

This politically stagnant period would last until the timely appearance of Joan of Arc. Meanwhile, a few signs pointed to some hope for the House of Valois. First, in December 1424, Philip the Good, Duke of Burgundy, gave his sister Agnes in marriage to the Count of Clermont, an ardent Armagnac and Orléans loyalist. This union could never have been approved had the Duke of Burgundy wanted to continue his alliance with England; his pointed absence from Paris followed by the wedding of his sister to the "enemy" was an overt snub aimed at Bedford. He further distanced himself from the English sphere by spending more and more time in Ghent and Bruges, hardly visiting his Burgundian capital at Dijon.

The second event brightening the horizons of the French king was a storm brewing in London. In 1421, the Duke of Gloucester had been named regent in England by his brother King Henry V and became a guardian of the baby, King Henry VI with their uncle, the Duke of Beaufort (who was also the Bishop of Winchester and later Cardinal). Upon Gloucester's return to England after his failed attempt to capture the Low Counties, he found his uncle

Beaufort ready to take over. Beaufort's troops were in control of the Tower of London, and his kingdom was on the brink of civil war. The Duke of Bedford left Paris in December 1425 to quell the palace revolt and remained in London for 16 months, until the spring of 1427. In his absence his English troops on the continent did nothing, which was an unexpected boon to the French, who were still in a state of disarray since their defeat at Verneuil.

The Duke of Bedford found the English in England divided on many counts, and especially in their support of the war in France. The majority of the noblemen and wealthy merchants were enthusiastic to add the vast dominions of France to their own crown, but the tax-burdened masses were complaining of the heavy costs of the seemingly endless war. Bedford named himself Regent of England, promised the English people a quick victory in exchange for financial support, and returned to France in March 1427. He was determined to invade and conquer the Valois strongholds of Maine and the Anjou; those countries would become his personal property. From there he would surround Bourges. The House of Valois would be eradicated.

Had Bedford been able to mobilize his troops immediately, he would have found the Royalist French immersed in a quagmire of internal dissidence, bordering on revolt. The feud between Arthur de Richemont and La Tremoille had grown into civil disruption, and Richemont had attempted to take the reins of power in Bourges by force in the spring of 1428. Unsuccessful, Richemont and his men were banished from court by Charles VII. The king was so completely under the egotistical influence of La Tremoille that his own judgment was nonexistent. Certain that he alone held the king's confidence, La Tremoille proposed a halt to all military operations and suggested instead ending the hostilities with England through diplomatic negotiations. That is all the Duke of Bedford would have needed for the quick victory he had promised his countrymen in London. Fortunately for King Charles, some patriotic Frenchmen were still loyal to the resistance. While the king's advisers were feuding, Charles Dunois and Etienne de Vignolle, called La Hire, led their small army in combat, and in the name of King Charles VII successfully took the towns of Montargis and Montdoubleau on the far outskirts of Paris. At the same time an English fleet of 120 small ships was captured by Breton corsairs from St. Malo led by Bernard de Kerqualen. The years of inactivity were over, and the warring armies began to prepare once more for battle.

In June 1428, John Montaigu, the Earl of Salisbury, landed at Calais with an army of 6,000 men. After conferring with the duke of Bedford, Lord Salisbury joined his newly arrived troops with 6,000 of the English soldiers already garrisoned in Normandy and, as the new commander of the English forces, began his march toward Maine and Anjou. Bedford had wanted the army to then head straight for Bourges and lay siege to the Royalist capital, but Salisbury and his lieutenants—Lords Talbot and Scales—insisted that taking the Loire city of Orléans would be the key to breaking the enemy forces. Bedford demurred to these military tacticians and moved to Chartres, where he set up his personal headquarters to be nearer the field of action.

Action was one-sided. In little more than a month almost every village and town on their route toward Orléans had capitulated in the face of this mighty army on the move. The town of Chateaudun alone withstood the English forces, and Salisbury didn't linger there; he was eager to reach his goal. Beaugency soon fell to the English and then Meung, Jargeau, Marche-Noir, and Notre Dame de Clery. King Henry VI's army arrived outside Orléans on October 12, 1428, bearing the standards of both houses, Lancaster and Valois. Lord Salisbury immediately began to prepare the siege that would become one of the most memorable in history.

The English were well-prepared, and well-paid, with foot soldiers and lancers receiving sixpence a day and archers and artillerymen a shilling. They were eager for battle. Charles VII was at the Chateau de Chinon, only forty miles away, in a state of abject melancholy as the daily reports arrived. The unwritten laws of chivalry forbade attack on the private property of a prisoner of war. Salisbury chose to ignore tradition when he selected Orléans as his target for siege, fully aware that Charles of Orléans was still held captive in London and unable to defend his fief.

But the people of Orléans were proud loyalists and the absence of their lord gave them even more spirited determination to withstand the English attack. For weeks, before October 12, the Orléanais were busy day and night stockpiling wheat, oil, wood, arms, and munitions behind the pale-yellow walls of the city.

Orléans was well-fortified, surrounded as it was by a high, thick crenellated stone wall, sloping slightly inward, with more than thirty lookout towers, all re-enforced by the Orléanais some fifteen years earlier. The entire ancient city had been built on the northern bank of the widest part of the Loire, and the medieval fortified Orléans was connected by one single drawbridge to a great seventeen-arch bridge that spanned the Loire to its southern bank. On this bridge, at midway over the Loire, stood a tiny one-room defense tower named after Saint Anthony. Another, larger bastion with twin towers, called The Tournelles, had been erected at the spot where the bridge met the southern bank. A few hundred meters still further stood the Augustinian Fort, an enclosed fortress holding a garrison of Orléanais soldiers.

The English were camped in a semicircular formation, from riverbank to riverbank, all around the city on the northern shore. Twelve thousand English soldiers were on the alert, lying in wait for the city to crumble from within and capitulate. Lord Salisbury and Lord Talbot were just a few miles away, at the chateaux they had sequestered for their military headquarters. They fully expected the siege to have succeeded by Christmas.

The Royalists still held their defense on the southern bank, and access to the beleaguered city remained open. Charles Dunois, the bastard son of Orléans and half-brother of the captive duke, arrived with a small army to direct operations from within. The bridge was crucial to their survival, as convoys after convoy of carts and wagons delivered the supplies that would keep the Orléanais alive through the dire months ahead.

On October 17, after hours of hand-to-hand combat in which even some women of the city fought with picks and axes, the English took the Augustiani Fort and Les Tournelles; the bridge was theirs. The English would cease their fire and wait, certain that the inhabitants were destined to starve; when that time came, King Henry VI's troops would march into Orléans and the city would be theirs. The rest of the Loire Valley would follow.

But Dubois blew the bridge. The English enemies couldn't march into the city, but now the people of Orléans were absolutely isolated. It would be next to impossible to supply the defenders with more food or munitions. It was just a question of time.

Lord Salisbury was killed on October 24, hit in the head by a stone that ricocheted off one of the towers of Les Tournelles as he stood there observing the south bank. This was a great blow to the English and a boon to the French; Salisbury was known to be one of the best military strategists in all of England. Lord Salisbury was immediately replaced by the Earl of Suffolk, who had been freed on ransom, and English determination rose. More English troops marched through France toward Orléans, and many French families welcomed their arrival, raising toasts to the health of Henry VI, who was just seven years old. It was becoming common thought that, after all, the long war was nothing more than a family feud. Wasn't little Henry's mother, Catherine, the daughter of a French king?

More than all others Yolande d'Aragon and Richemont realized how much the future of France rested on Charles's weak shoulders. That is perhaps why many French historians credit Yolande, given her connections with the House of Lorraine, with the arrival of Joan of Arc at Chinon.

In October 1428 King Charles VII was living at the Chateau de Chinon, the most massive of his royal residences. In the face of impending peril to his throne, King Charles had called for a meeting of his Estates General, or parliament, and the deputies readily agreed to raise the sum of 400,000 pounds to mount yet another army to defend Orléans. No one except beggars and the church was exempt from this call to service, and once more the exhausted French lifted their banners and prepared for battle.

Throughout November and December the enemy troops under the command of Lords Suffolk, Talbot, and Scales reinforced their positions on the northern bank of the Loire and built hundreds of bunkers all around the northern side of the city walls. Their work was progressing slowly and the southern flank was still not protected; small quantities of supplies were still being sneaked into the city during moonless nights. The defenseless and heroic Orléanais were led by their able bailiff, Raoul de Gaucourt, but after three months of siege food supplies were low and winter had just begun.

In January 1429, Charles Dubois escaped from Orléans and met with King Charles VII at Blois. It was concluded that their only hope was to play for time and the best way to do that would be to intercept fresh supplies en route to Suffolk's men.

Small Royalist forces had already been harassing the English convoys for weeks on their way from Chartres to Orléans to try to deflate enemy morale. In February 1429, during Lent, the Royalists and their king were dealt an enormous blow. It became known as the unfortunate Day of the Herrings.

About three hundred wagons carrying tons of salted herrings in barrels to Suffolk's troops, accompanied by 1,500 English soldiers, left Chartres on February 9. Three Royalist armies were meant to converge simultaneously at a given spot and destroy the wagons and their cargo, but everything that could go wrong did go wrong. First, the English were forewarned of the impending attack and, near Rouvrau-Saint-Denis, formed the heavily loaded wagons into a huge circle with troops in the middle. Then, the three armies, led by Dubois, Clermont, and the Scot John Stuart, failed to attack simultaneously. The intended trap was a total fiasco for the French. John Stuart was killed in the field, Dunois was wounded, and Clermont never entered into the fight. Wagons were overturned, everybody reeked of fish, and only La Hire and Xantrailles would save the armies by leading a somewhat orderly retreat. Once more the disunity of the French forces had cost them a victory. The French cause was approaching collapse.

Dunois, La Hire, and Xantrailles were of the minor nobility; they had neither fiefs nor chateaux and few of their officers owned their own suits of armor. Fortunately they were energetic, intelligent, and adventurous, and although, like so many others, they dominated Charles by their strong personalities, they were entirely loyal to a cause in which they believed.

Charles was, by birth if not by character or inclination, the titular head of that cause. The king was still at the Chateau de Chinon, profoundly distressed and withdrawn. The brave people of Orléans were running out of food and munitions. The only thing that kept them from surrendering to the English was the idea of the aftermath of surrender. They preferred death by cold and starvation to the unthinkable violent fate they would suffer at the hands of the English army.

The situation was abysmal. Charles once again considered exile, and noblemen began to fortify their personal property. Only a miracle could change the swelling tide of English victory.

CHAPTER TEN

According to George Bordonove, the excellent French historian, one has to visit Domremy in order to better understand Joan of Arc and her role in history. Domremy is a particularly pretty village in the Lorraine, not far from the source of the River Meuse, which runs through it. Joan's girlhood house is still standing near the church in the center of Domremy, and apparently the surrounding countryside has changed little over the past 500 years. It is a soft and romantic landscape with rolling hills, wide green pastures, and great oak trees, at once inspiring and restful.

Joan was born in Domremy in about 1412, to descendants of freed serfs who owned and tilled their own ten or so acres of land. Her parents, Pierre of Arc and Isabelle were devout loyalists, like the other people in the region. Joan and her three older brothers and younger sister grew up hearing stories of their poor young king. The children were unlettered (Joan would say later when she was grilled by members of the clergy that she knew "neither A nor B"), and they took turns herding the village sheep to pasture. It was in these pastures that Joan first heard the celestial voices that would eventually guide her to her destiny. The voices spoke to her frequently over a period of five or six years. During these years she spoke of the visitations to no one, but she finally confided to her uncle that Saint Margaret and Saint Catherine, the Archangel Gabriel, and Saint Michael were all urging her on behalf of God toward a divine mission to defend the king and the crown. Within weeks word spread that God had chosen a young shepherdess to save France. Joan and her uncle were received by a local nobleman, Robert de Baudricourt, who was dubious at first but was finally convinced of her sincere piety by clergymen from the region. Furthermore, an old French prophecy said that one day France would be lost by a woman and saved by a virgin. Was Isabel de Bavière that woman? Could Joan be the savior? Prophets, mystics, and seers were commonplace during the Middle Ages, but even in a century rife with prophecies, Joan of Arc stood out with her energetic sense of purpose.

The Duke of Lorraine, suffering from ill health, heard of Joan and sent for her. The people of Domremy offered her a horse, and accompanied by her uncle and brothers, Joan met with the duke in his chateau in Nancy. She apparently told him that the only way to cure his illness was to stop sleeping with his mistress. The duke gave up his mistress, his health improved, and Joan returned to Domremy, her status much enhanced following her reception at the court of Lorraine.

Baudricourt received her once again, in February 1429, at about the time of the herring affair. Joan was impatient to see the king himself, and Orléans was desperately near capitulation. Outfitted by Baudricourt in men's clothing for safer travel, Joan arrived in Chinon on March 6.

Several theories have been raised as to the authenticity of Joan: Was she an illegitimate child delivered to a couple of peasants? Was she the daughter of Isabeau, thus sister of the king, who had difficulties reigning? These are not very different—though far-fetched—from the myths of the birth of Zeus, Romulus and Remus, or Oedipus, in which the character is the son of a king or a queen, hidden at birth by a faithful wet nurse, and entrusted to a peasant family. It is entirely possible that Yolande d'Aragon was present in Nancy during Joan's visit to the Lorraine capital. Another theory is that Yolande may have asked Joan to pretend to hear voices, convinced that this may pave the way to save the crown!

The second Anjou son, René, the future King of Naples, was married to the Duke of Lorraine's eldest daughter and his heir. Yolande kept very close contact with all her children and often visited the Court of Lorraine. She was at Chinon when Joan of Arc presented herself at the castle gates, and the insightful lady became the champion of Joan's cause. At first Charles refused to see her, but Joan was adamant that God had sent her with an urgent message that she must deliver to the king herself. Yolande convinced her son-in-law that the young maiden dressed as a man was not a simple prophetess who wished only to pray for the king, but also an extraordinary seer who was prepared to give her life for France. On her third day at Chinon Joan was admitted to the Great Hall of the castle, the walls of which still stand to remind us of that fateful day. Charles VII was dissimulated as a courtier, milling among the crowds thronging the hall for the event. Another courtier, dressed as the king, sat on the throne near the door at the end of the room, but Joan, ignoring the imposter, walked straight to Charles VII, kneeled down before him, and announced,

"Sire, God has sent me to you to tell you that you are the son of the king and the true heir to the throne of France!" There, in front of several hundred witnesses, Joan called him the son of the king, as Yolande had called him twenty years before, and these were words Charles had longed to hear again. The visionary shepherdess was only seventeen, but she had the confidence that Charles was lacking, and she awakened him to the possibility of future glory. Although anxious and somewhat doubtful, the king wasn't indifferent to the passionate and outspoken young peasant girl. Later during a private audience Charles asked for a sign to prove his legitimacy. Joan replied that the sign would be victory at Orléans.

Mistrusting as ever, Charles VII asked theologians from all over the region to question the young girl, and Joan replied favorably, although in a somewhat cocky manner, to their myriad questions concerning her faith, the voices, and her intentions. Together Yolande and Joan went to Poitiers, where Joan underwent further interrogation and a medical examination by a midwife that proved that she was, indeed, a virgin. Virginity was then indisputable evidence that no pact with the devil had been consummated, thus proof in Joan's case that she was not a witch. Unfortunately, this was overlooked by the judges in her later trials.

For the time being, the entire royal court was satisfied with Joan's claims, her moral honesty having fended off even the most skeptical doubters. The people of Orléans could hardly hold out much longer and Charles reconsidered his options; perhaps the strange young maiden was Heaven sent.

Wearing her new suit of armor and glinting sword, flying her own embroidered standard of Christ between two angels, Joan left Chinon to join what was left of the army at Blois. The Duke of Alençon rallied to her call for troops, and so did Xantrailles, La Hire, Gilles de Rais, and other brave and experienced men of war. The Marshall de Boussac was commander of the operation, and Joan rode on her white horse, at the head of the army, by Boussac's side. She was radiant with confidence and behaved more like a captain than the simple source of inspiration she was meant to be. Arriving at Orléans with a vanguard of troops on April 29, 1429, Joan entered the city by ladder and was received "like an angel from Heaven" by the starving Orléanais. Dunois, governor of Orléans, and the courageous bailiff-captain de Gaucourt had despaired of help; a few days more and the city would be lost.

By May 4, most of the French army had assembled around Orléans and on the outskirts of the south bank. The English naturally expected attack to come from the south but were surprised from the north where their defense was weak. The French troops had crossed the Loire upriver and had circled around. It was an easy first victory for the French. Once the French were certain that the enemy supply route was cut, they concentrated their attacks from the south, and on May 6 took the Augustinian Fort, led in battle by Joan.

The English were incredulous as they retreated for a night of rest. Their plans had gone awry, they had lost each battle for three consecutive days, their supply lines were cut, and the whole siege had been for nothing, all because of a peasant girl!

On the morning of May 7, the French captains found their troops too tired for battle and declared a day of rest. Once defenders, the Royalist troops had become the attackers, and now the English were on the defense, but Joan, upon hearing this plan for rest, insisted on the importance of routing the English from their last stronghold, Les Tournelles. Her energy and confidence shamed the weary soldiers into action, and she personally ordered and led the attack. At dawn on May 7, the French surrounded Les Tournelles, and never before had the French troops fought with more determination. The English, however, were not about to cede their only foothold south of the Loire, and they put up a bitter fight. Early in the afternoon Joan was wounded in the shoulder by an arrow and was removed from the front for treatment. While she was recovering, Dunois approached to tell her that he thought they should stop the attack and begin again the following morning. The thought of even one night's withdrawal from battle revived the wounded girl; after a few moments of solitary prayer, Joan leaped back into the fray, darting here and there to give words of encouragement to the soldiers. Within a few hours under her frenetic leadership, they had wiped out the English. The Loire was littered with hundreds of dead bodies, and many English soldiers had drowned trying to escape across the river. Les Tournelles gave the French their first victory of such a magnitude, and the English commanders who had witnessed the battle were in a state of shock.

Joan, or the Maid of Orléans as she would henceforth be called, Dunois, La Hire, and the other officers spent the night of May 7 plotting the battle plans for the following day. The bells of the churches of Orléans tolled all night long, and by dawn of May 8 the French armies were in battle formation, ready to meet the English counterattack. The English forces also were in formation, but to the utter disbelief of every Orléanais and French soldier, the entire English army turned and marched away from Orléans. Until today, the Orléanais celebrate annually the French victory and the liberation of Orléans on May 8, 1429.

The Maid of Orléans, Le Hire, Dunois, and Xantrailles met with a jubilant King Charles VII three days later at the Chateau of Loches, where Charles was residing. The English army had retreated to Jargeau, under the command of the Earl of Suffolk. The Maid of Orléans and her brave companions spent a month in Gien, regrouping their own forces. On June 12, the French army took Jargeau with few losses. The English retreated to Patay. Unexpectedly, Arthur de Richemont arrived to join the Royalists with 1,500 archers and lancers of his own and, in spite of his quarrel with the king, his aid was welcome. Joan, once again riding at the head of what she had come to consider "her" army, routed the English at Patay. English losses were heavy: Two thousand men died at Patay, and the Lords Suffolk, Talbot, and Scales were taken prisoner. English morale was at its lowest ebb; wherever Joan fought, the English had been beaten and taken prisoner and their soldiers were afraid of her.

Chapter Eleven

Charles's mother-in-law held some influence over him, but her many duties claimed most of her time and she could see him only occasionally. Each time she returned from mission abroad Yolande did her best to counsel Charles and encourage him, and for a while after her visits he seemed inclined to follow her sage advice. But his bad habits and vice-ridden entourage triumphed over his weak resolve and he unfailingly fell back into the immoral depths of his new associations. After having spent days alone, morose and apathetic, the king would join his raucous friends in a month-long frenzy of gambling, drinking, and womanizing, and he spent frequent and longer periods away from his family, most often at his chateau in Chinon. Whether in an insular or rambunctious mood, Charles never behaved like a king who was living on the edge of the abyss and never made any move to indicate that he was coping with problems of state. The people were beginning to say that Charles had inherited his father's mental frailty.

His favorites, debauched and intriguing as they were, sometimes tried to kill one another in the hope of becoming closer to the king. When they didn't kill each other Charles's old tutor the Count of Richemont would do it for them, as in the case of Pierre de Giac.

Giac was a dashing and handsome wild man of particularly sinister and unscrupulous character and was said to have made a pact with the devil himself. One of the murderers of the Duke of Burgundy on the Montereau bridge, he had long been the lover of Queen Isabel; having reduced the queen's treasury by as much as he could, he moved on to Charles's at Chinon court. Greatly admired by the king, who made him First Lord Chamberlain, Giac took over the palace and installed his own "King's Guard" of about 150 rowdy men who fought duels, brought an endless stream of vulgar women to the court, and stabbed each other to death during drunken brawls. They kidnapped for ransom, they plundered the countryside, and they generally made the court appear as headquarters for evil rabble-rousing pirates.

It was at this time that Giac met a rich and beautiful widow, the Countess Catherine de Tonnerre, whom he wished to marry immediately; but first he had to consider his own wife, who was seven months with child. He found his solution after first confessing openly with Satan: Rushing home the same night he forced his wife to drink poison, tied her with a long rope to his horse, dragged her at a gallop for fifteen miles, then buried her on the spot by the light of the moon. Three weeks later he married Catherine. The all-powerful Giac underestimated the will of Yolande, who arrived at Charles's court, now lodged at the chateau of Issoudun, accompanied by Richemont. Giac was pulled from his bed by Richemont's guards, given a quick trial, and sentenced to death by drowning. Although he offered 100,000 Ecus for his deliverance and to give over all his men as hostages, Pierre de Giac was tied up in a bag and thrown into the river.

Georges de la Tremoille, another past favorite of Queen Isabel, watched the execution from the river bank. A few days later he was First Lord Chamberlain, and the following month he married Catherine Giac.

Loyal Richemont was too brutally frank to endear himself to the insecure king; Tremoille was the sort of man Charles admired. Rich, powerful, and a clever strategist, Tremoille could have been an enormous asset to the crown, but unfortunately for Charles, Tremoille was working only for himself. When Richemont returned to court a few months later he found a despotic Tremoille ruling single-handedly, unwilling to listen to counsel. Charles was subjugated by the forceful interloper, perhaps thinking that some of Tremoille's ferocious strength would become his own.

Yolande d'Aragon tried to reason with the king: He was in danger of losing whatever little was left of the crown; the vassals still loyal to the Valois were diminishing in number, and Charles was still only King of Bourges and little else. Yolande tried to enlist the help of her daughter Marie, but the submissive and resigned little queen wrote back, "He is my lord—while he has a right over any of my actions, I have none over his."

Orléans was delivered on May 8, and Joan, riding at the head of a proud and jubilant army, met with the king in Tours three days later, where they spent a week together. It was often questioned how a peasant girl could mount so nobly on a horse, sword in hand. In fact, later on, during her grilling by the inquisition, she had clearly said never having used her sword!

Explaining her sacred mission to the king, the Maid of Orléans saw herself as leading a crusade, not simply an army, and would not rest until every last English soldier had left France. She was enthusiastic to accompany the king to Orléans so that he could see the joy of his loyal subjects and then on to Reims for his consecration. Mistrusting and aloof as ever, Charles was nevertheless grateful, so reluctantly he agreed to her plan. Loyal followers of Charles assembled their newly inspired armies behind the king and the maid in Gien at the end of June 1429 and they began their march north toward the cathedral in Reims. All along the way cities, towns, and villages, so long under English domination, acclaimed Charles as their one and only king. Arriving at Reims Charles was greeted by his brother-in-law, René d'Anjou, now Duke of Lorraine. Together they received the notables of the city, who had come to swear their allegiance to the king. The king recorded in his journal that this show of loyalty was very moving to him. Charles pardoned the people of Reims for past alliances with the Anglo-Burgundian forces. Following this meeting, it was decided not to waste any time—the coronation would take place the next day, Sunday, July 17, 1429. During an arduous ceremony that began at nine in the morning and lasted until two o'clock in the afternoon, Charles was anointed and crowned with a modest crown borrowed from the cathedral treasury; the crown of Charlemagne, traditionally worn by French kings, was locked in the Basilica of Saint-Denis, still in English hands.

Overnight, Charles changed. The malingering kinglet became radiant and majestic. He received a delegation of Burgundians in the afternoon following his sacrament and tentatively agreed to a peace treaty. Annoyed by Joan of Arc's insistence to continue to fight until France was wholly French, Charles avoided her as much as he could, determined to negotiate peace through diplomacy. He returned to his beloved Loire Valley; he was king and that was enough to satisfy him for the time being.

Far away in Ivry, Richemont continued to act on behalf of the king; he was never the courtesan, always the patriot. La Tremoille, however, would remain at the center of the royal court for six years as chief flatterer and master of intrigue.

The king and his followers had moved from the king's chateau at Loches to Sully-sur-Loire, the domain belonging to La Tremoille. It was here that Joan, accompanied by the Duke of Alençon, met with the king in late June to try to convince him that his immediate priority was to proceed for the holy sacrament and traditional coronation in that city's ancient cathedral. In turn La Tremoille did his best to convince Charles that the far better route to take would be the one to Normandy to chase the English armies across the Channel. It was clearly premature to attempt an offense of that scale in Normandy, but such was La Tremoille's influence over the king that he remained uncertain and undecided for days. The Maid of Orléans, however, was adamant about her voices and their orders, and Charles eventually and reluctantly agreed to go to Reims.

Simon Charles, president of the king's Chambers Accounts, narrates a touching episode evoking the march toward Reims: "I heard from the mouth of the king some very kind words about Joan. It was at Saint-Benoit-sur-Loire. The king, pitying Joan for the pains she was enduring, ordered her to rest. She then told the king not to doubt, that he would soon have his whole kingdom, and that he would be crowned." Joan has only one issue in her mind, the mission that has been given to her, and her first aim is to see the king crowned.

Leaving Reims on July 22, King Charles rode toward Paris. It was the hope of the Maid of Orléans that Charles would enter the capital and, taking advantage of the disarray in the English forces, take the city without a fight.

Although still under the influence of La Tremoille, he was nevertheless king, and that was enough to satisfy him for the time being. On August 28, as King of France, he signed a temporary truce with Jean of Luxembourg, who was acting on behalf of the Duke of Burgundy. The truce restricted the king's right to enter any part of France north of the Seine and was in other ways disadvantageous to the Royalists, but La Tremoille advised him to stall for time; after all, the truce was only temporary.

Eventually poor Joan became a nuisance to him, nearly hysterical in her crusade to rid France of its enemies. In the name of King Charles VII she engaged in small battles here and skirmishes there, zealously training new troops whenever she found troops to train, until she was captured, just a year after her great victory, by Burgundy's men. From then on she was moved from prison to prison and shown off as the Burgundian's prize. Sold to the English four months later for 10,000 Ecus, she was taken to Rouen and tried for heresy. On Wednesday morning, May 30, 1431, at nine o'clock, she was delivered to her executors before the huge crowds surrounding three great tribunals erected around the market square. Mounting the scaffold in the center of the square she asked a priest nearby to hold his cross high so that she might see it. Engulfed by crackling flames, her last cry was "Jesus!" It took four hours for her body to burn to ashes, which were then thrown unceremoniously into the Seine to ensure that no relic would remain of the martyr. John Tussard, a secretary to the king of England, watched the execution from a tribunal and later that day wrote: "We are lost as it is a good and saintly woman that was burned."

She was quickly forgotten, virtually ignored by historians for more than four hundred years and only given sainthood in 1912. Joan of Arc was merely a glorious incident in the life of Charles VII. During the entire year of her imprisonment the king never once made the least effort to intercede on her behalf. Just how cold and shallow he was is evident in his reaction to the news of her cruel execution: Interrupted while playing cards he said, "Oh well, there was something of a witch about her."

Newly inspired armies were born out of the maid's dream of victory, and carrying the standard of the House of Valois they cleared away what remained of the joint English and Burgundian army in the south. With his enemies now so far away, the king had a newfound sense of importance, at least in the part of the country that had always been loyal to his cause.

Now it was English morale that was low. The Duke of Bedford, alarmed at the sudden change in the political climate, thought of a scheme: Henry VI should be crowned in Paris, encouraging a new wave of loyalty to the English king who had never visited France since his birth. At the end of November 1431, six months after the death of the Maid of Orléans, a small, shy, and nervous ten-year-old king rode into Paris accompanied by two thousand men in glittering armor. Ill at ease and with none of the physical attributes of the Plantagenets, the young English king looked very much like his uncle Charles VII. In spite of the triumphant arches and thousands of banners decorating the war-torn city, Paris was dismal under grey winter skies, and the masses cheering him along his route were thin and haggard. His coronation at Notre Dame was followed by eight days of sumptuous festivities attended by the clergy, the nobility, the bourgeoisie, the members of parliament and the University of Paris, and of course Henry's gaudy and aging grandmother, Isabel. The child king then returned to London, not having remained long enough for his visit to have been a positive effect on the population. Not a single Ecu had been spent on the poor, neither food nor wine was given to the masses; no amnesties were granted to prisoners, and as the last bits of bunting were taken down the disappointed Parisians were annoyed to see that their city would take second place to London.

No one was more aware of the hollow success of the coronation than the Duke of Bedford. It was slowly dawning on the French that they had been humiliated; they were not going to be joint partners in a new nation but simple serfs carrying the English breadbasket. Then in 1432 Bedford's wife died. As the sister of the young Duke of Burgundy she had been the link between the two powerful men who, outside their political alliance, now shared only their mutual hatred. The Duke of Bedford ignored Phillip the Good, and it was clear to the son of John the Fearless that their alliance had turned into English occupation. Neither as belligerent nor as Machiavellian as his father, he began to conceive of the future of France as French. Just a few months later Bedford remarried without deigning to forewarn Burgundy; this personal slight was the final straw in the dissolution of the English–Burgundian alliance.

Always alert to the possibility of an eventual Valois–Burgundy reconciliation, Yolande d'Aragon sent her emissaries to probe the political atmosphere
at the Burgundian court. They found Phillip the Good reconsidering his past
and his present; he felt betrayed by the English, and he was tired of war. When
the first tentative suggestions of peace were made by the count of Richemont,
Burgundy seemed open to the proposals.

At the same time many of the cities in the north were won over to King
Charles's side, and La Hire and Xantrailles marched triumphantly into the
Basilica of Saint-Denis, where they were joyfully acclaimed by the masses.

The tide was turning, and although young Burgundy was decided in his
heart to end the conflict, he was nevertheless unwilling to lose the autonomy
particular to the House of Burgundy. The first attempts to hold a peace conference ended without success, but at last the conference opened at Arras on July
1, 1435, and was attended by most of the ruling houses of Europe: The kings
of Poland, Portugal and Denmark were present, as were the Kings of Navarre,
Castille, and Aragon. The pope and other princely houses sent ambassadors to
represent them. Phillip the Good came in person, but King Charles did not
attend; among the many who represented the House of France were the Duke
of Bourbon, the Count of Richemont, and the Chancellor Regnault of Chartres. The English king remained in England but sent a large delegation led by
the bishops of York, Norwich, and Saint-Davids and the lords Suffolk and
Holland. The proposals for peace made on behalf of King Henry VI were
English sovereignty with recognition of Charles's rights south of the Loire as
dauphin, marriage between Henry and one of Charles VII's daughters, and a
forty-year truce. These proposals were immediately declared unacceptable by
the congress; the English withdrew from the conference and left Arras en
masse. But the conference went on.

Essentially both King Charles and the Duke of Burgundy wanted peace.
After the noisy departure of the English deputation Phillip the Good received
Charles's representatives at his table and made clear his desire for reconciliation with his cousin, but he stalled over some of the fine points of the peace
treaty. Negotiation was slowing down when they learned that the Duke of
Bedford had died in Paris on September 14. Aware that the unknown could be
worse than the familiar, Phillip the Good was suddenly eager for a permanent
alliance and the preliminaries to the Treaty of Arras were drawn up within the
week.

In the first article of the treaty, and this was very much a major issue,
Charles agreed to make amends for the murder of John the Fearless by building a chapel and monastery next to the bridge of Montereau. He further
pledged to give John's son full autonomy during his lifetime over his possessions of Burgundy, Flanders, and Franche-Conté and to pay half a million

Ecus to Burgundy as indemnity. The Duke of Burgundy in turn recognized King Charles as his only sovereign and promised never to make a separate peace with the King of England.

Isabel of Bavaria did not live to see the final peace. The wretched queen died in Paris on September 4, 1435. No one cared. Slatternly, obese, and disregarded by everyone, she died alone. Her corpse, accompanied by four palace servants, was transported by barge to Saint-Denis and buried without ceremony in the basilica next to her husband's tomb.

The final Treaty of Arras was signed by King Charles, the Dauphin Louis, and the Duke of Burgundy before the entire congress on December 10th, 1435. It was celebrated in the Cathedral of Arras and all over again in the Cathedral of Bourges, followed by great masses of thanksgiving held all over France. Heralds were dispatched to London to announce the tidings to King Henry VI, who with the childish petulance that characterized the boy of fourteen, wept openly, crying over and over, "I've lost my French kingdom!" It was a bitter pill for the English to swallow.

It is said that much later, in 1456, King Charles VII—possibly through Agnès's influence, years earlier—may have pardoned and rehabilitated Joan of Arc, giving her the title of "Jeanne dame de Lys." However, there is no record of an inch of land having been conferred to her, which was the local custom. The king would have linked her to his kingdom and the nation, but because she had vows of chastity and poverty, he did not give her any terrestrial benefits. The d'Arc family remained common people.

CHAPTER TWELVE

Finally, Agnès appears! The name Agnès in French is a pretty romantic name—not like the English Agnes!

At the middle of the fifteenth century, printing was at its beginning. Biographies were unknown, so the mystery surrounding Agnès during her six years with the king turned to legend. It is thanks to the chroniclers' manuscripts and a few surviving letters and diaries that some of the legends were transformed into historical fact. Although there are no existing documents giving her precise date and place of birth, Agnès was probably born in 1422, in Picardy, near the banks of the Oise. The Maignelais were defenders of the king in the region of Compiègne. She was not born in Touraine as some say, nor in Froitmantel or Fromenteau!

Her aristocratic family dates from the tenth century in the north of France, and many of her ancestors, with such names as Thorole and Raineval, played important roles during the Crusades. She was the first of five children and the only daughter of Jean Sorel, lord of Coudon and Saint-Gerant and advisor to the Count of Clermont, and his wife, Catherine de Maignelais, herself the Chatelaine of Vermeuil. The Sorel and Maignelais families were known to be partisans of the Valois cause and, living as they did in the midst of Burgundian territory in the north of France, they sent Agnès to the Touraine to live with her maternal aunt. The aunt, Madame de Magnelais, loved Agnès and brought her up as her own daughter. The little we know of Agnès's childhood is that she was beautiful and intelligent and of sweet and thoughtful temperament. Madame de Magnelais had a daughter of her own, Antoinette, who was about Agnès's age. Antoinette was, her mother bemoans, of a jealous nature, not pretty, and full of "sentiments not as noble and not as pure as our Agnès." One can only imagine that if Agnès had any problems as a child they must have come from Antoinette.

An affectionate child (as one chronicler with hindsight later wrote, "made for love,"), Agnès was given the education typical to a young girl of aristocratic birth. As most noble girls of her age, Agnès would have learned to embroider and play a musical instrument. She also would have had the practical training of running a household, raising children, and the rudiments of nursing for the sick because a girl's education was preparation for one single goal: marriage. Although girls didn't ordinarily study philosophy or mathematics, they learned enough arithmetic with the abacus to be able to keep accounts, and they learned to read and write, as Agnès did, with proficiency; her own penmanship was smooth and graceful. Religious education was of great importance and many sacred teachings were copied in the vernacular, sparing pious young girls the need to learn to read Latin. Robert de Blois, master of etiquette, had written a guide during the thirteenth century, which had been copied thousands of times and was still followed two hundred years later; Agnès and her cousin probably knew it by heart, the do's and the don'ts of polite conversation, dress, makeup, and personal hygiene. There was a certain level of cultural knowledge required by a woman of the upper class. Music; poetry, especially the chivalric epics; and art were subjects important to woman's conversation, and Agnès would have been well-versed in these subjects, as most educated girls were.

Throughout her childhood Agnès was always referred to as a great beauty of exceptional intelligence, and by the time she was fourteen her reputation as a young prodigy of sorts had spread even beyond the limits of the Touraine. Many of the great of the land travelled to Madame de Maignelais' chateau de Fromanteau to have a look for themselves; the Duke d'Alençon and Charles de Bourbon were among the hundreds of visitors. All opinions concur that she was of a beauty rarely seen, and all descriptions of her are similar. Her hair was blonde, of several shades from ash to gold "which comes into its full glory only in the sunlight," and her skin is often described as "radiant" or "of an incomparable freshness" and compared to lilies and roses. Her eyes were large, almond-shaped, blue, and very expressive; the brow was "high and pure" and her lips were said by a contemporary to have been "deliciously designed." Even her teeth were perfectly even and white and she had the "attitude and gestures of a queen."

Apparently she was so overwhelmingly beautiful that visitors were occasionally struck dumb in her presence, then quickly put at ease by her own good manners, kindness, and spirited wit; she thus enjoyed a reputation for her sweet nature in addition to her breathtaking beauty. She came to be so widely admired for her grace and charm that Madame de Maignelais recognized that at fifteen Agnès was far too beautiful and intelligent to be wasted on a small corner of the Touraine; she arranged for her niece to enter the household of Isabel de Lorraine as lady-in-waiting.

Agnès took the news of her appointment very badly and tried desperately to change her aunt's mind, but the kindly chatelaine assured her young niece that living in an old chateau with an old lady was not in Agnès's best interests for her future. A few days later, in the spring of 1437, accompanied by her aunt, the reluctant young lady-in-waiting-to-be left her sheltered life at the Chateau de Maignelais for Nancy with its bustling northern population and busy city streets. In this immense new world and far from the mild climate of the Loire Valley, Agnès was received with kindness and affection in the palace of Isabel de Lorraine by the princess herself. They were to become devoted companions.

It was customary in France then, and for centuries to follow, that well-born young men and women, upon reaching adolescence, would leave their families and become attached to a larger and more powerful household in order to complete their worldly education. There, in new surroundings, the noble child entering into adulthood would observe the rules of public life in the company of other young men and women from similar backgrounds, serving and becoming apprentice to a member of a great family. In Agnès's case, she could hardly have attended a better school than the household of Isabel de Lorraine, the beautiful eldest daughter of Charles I, Duke of Lorraine, and Margaret of Bavaria. The duke, having no son, had assured the future of his fief by naming Isabel heir. The young Isabel, probably the most outstanding and talented princess of her century, had married René of Anjou, now King of Sicily, a marriage carefully arranged by his mother, the cool and clever dowager Yolande of Aragon. Lorraine thus became part of the house of Anjou and, as such, loyal to the Valois cause.

With this masterly political move the Queen of Sicily had multiplied the fortunes of her own kingdom and loyally served the crown of France at the same time. When Charles of Lorraine died in 1431, Isabel inherited the throne as planned, and her husband became popularly known as the Good King René; today, throughout France there are several children's songs about him. Admired for his paternal kindness to everyone, he was a gifted linguist and writer and painter, of which the poets of the day wrote exalted praise. A good soldier and benevolent king, he was perhaps a less astute politician than his perceptive wife, but they made a happy couple, a much admired one, and their court was merry, moral, and high regarded. Their palace was a meeting place for philosophers, historians, the clergy, nobility, and royalty from all over Europe and the Mediterranean, humming with festivities, jousts, balls, and banquets. Good King René was a bon vivant, and every event, however small, was cause enough for a celebration. Troubadours, minstrels, sculptors, painters, and poets flocked to Nancy as pilgrims to a sacred site, creating artistic and intellectual fusion, a Camelot in northern France.

Agnès thrived during her idyllic years in the rarefied atmosphere of the Lorraine–Anjou court. This cultural oasis in the midst of a vast wasteland was the model she would later emulate to reconstruct the court of the King of France. Observant and quick-witted, Agnès learned how to behave in every situation, and her sweetness and piety earned her friends and admirers from every walk of life; there is no record of any reprehensible thing she ever said or did. Her promising beauty of early adolescence had never outgrown itself, and literature of the time describing the composition of canon beauty as "whiteness of skin, tinged with pink, blondes of hair, harmonious features, oval face, high and regular nose, lively laughing eyes and fine vermilion lips" exactly fit contemporary descriptions of Agnès.

Makeup existed, having been worn in Europe from early feudal times, and face powder, creams, eyeliners, and lip stains were available to everyone. Any lady could have the vermilion lips so dear to the poets' hearts. According to Henri de Mondeville, a chronicler of the thirteenth century, women exchanged recipes for creams, scents, and depilatory wax. Particularly important were various concoctions made to mask body odors and make the hair, which was worn long and untied, fragrant, using musk, cloves, nutmeg, cardamom, and other valuable spices from the east. He advised ladies to wear crowns of roses and eglantine when in close contact with a gentleman and to sweeten their breath with fennel, cumin, and anise seeds. His other advice was more direct: "While making love never allow yourself to be kissed, for disagreeable odors become more so when you are hot."

Contraception was already an ancient practice by the fifteenth century. Marital infidelity was commonplace among the nobility, its general acceptance having begun during the Crusades and reaching its apogee during the fifteenth century with the advent of romantic poetry. Sodomy and coitus interruptus were common methods used to prevent unwanted pregnancy, but local witches had their own prescriptions: specially brewed magical herbal lathers or heated sheep uterus used as a protective lining.

People were generally cleaner in France during the fifteenth and sixteenth centuries than in later French history. Most families had a bathtub, usually long and deep and made of tin, and bathing was a ritual accorded with the lunar calendar: The ninth day after the new moon, for instance, was considered a good day for a bath! A bath was also part of the rites of welcome; a family receiving a visitor would offer him a hot bath to refresh him after his journey. But frequent baths were reserved for the nobility; only they had the time and space and the necessary help to heat water, fill the tub, and bathe in privacy. It is known that Agnès bathed every day; her bath water was sweetened with essences. When she travelled her large tin bath, carried by mule cart, went everywhere with her.

By the early 1440s, Agnès's fame had spread throughout France; she was known as Belle Agnès. Not a ranking lady-in-waiting, she was nevertheless a favorite companion of Isabel de Lorraine and accompanied her patron everywhere, maturing into an accomplished, gracious, and clever young lady. Why wasn't she married? That was supposed to be every young woman's goal. Perhaps she was too happy at the Lorraine court to consider changing her way of life—after all, she had been sent to Nancy to learn how to run a household, but she had learned instead to run a palace. Perhaps her dowry was too insignificant to attract a husband she would find suitable; she was from a family of little importance, and marriages were still arranged with mutual benefits in mind. The minor noblemen of her own lower-down-the-ladder social rank could be of no interest to her as husbands. Then, perhaps it was simply destiny that preserved her for her great role in French history.

However well-considered for her virtues, morality, and piety, it is unlikely that the Belle Agnès remained a virgin during her seven years in the service of Isabel of Lorraine. A very strict double standard dated from the earliest feudal times, and the basis of it was a man's honor. This did not mean women were dishonored; women basically represented temptation and a man was bound by reputation to take the tempting female, thus maintaining his honor. This seems very hocus-pocus by today's standards, and even then many women gave themselves freely, but the beautiful young maiden who had been seduced by a chivalrous knight was not diminished in the eyes of others; she was simply playing her expected role. Agnès was nearly 22 when she met the king; as a ravishing beauty living in the merry court of Lorraine it is impossible that she was not seduced by an honorable knight or two. The House of Lorraine-Anjou was a convivial setting that attracted good-looking youth from all over Europe in a new age of songs and poems of illicit love; a little promiscuity was unavoidable when dozens of young men and women lived together under the same roof.

Agnès and the court of Lorraine, although isolated from the miserable realities in the rest of France, had news from travelers, letters, and an occasional copy of the *Paris Gazette,* a hand-copied forerunner of a modern daily newspaper. There were no minstrels nor painters in Paris; great entertainment was a tournament in which four blind men carrying clubs beat one another while trying to kill a pig running loose among them. Unabated violence and disease had taken a heavy toll: The population of Paris, 200,000 in 1400, was decimated by 1440; there were reports of cannibalism and more than 5,000 beggars lived on the streets. France had been at war with England, and often with itself, since anyone alive could remember and there was no end in sight.

CHAPTER THIRTEEN

Charles VII was, at last, considered the rightful King of France by his subjects and now, in his early thirties, he could begin to build a future for his realm based on a solid foundation: his recognized legitimacy to rule.

A great many of his most fearful enemies had died and become ghosts of his past. His parents and brothers were dead, as were Henry V and the Duke of Bedford. He could begin to feel confident about his future and that of his country. Most of the positive forces and guiding lights of his youth were still alive and still loyal, albeit from a distance.

One by one they re-introduced themselves into his new life after the death of Joan of Arc. Yolande d'Aragon, Arthur de Richemont, and even Tanguy du Chatel rejoined the king's inner circle during the early 1430s, and Charles VII was grateful.

The rowdy group of parasites that still constituted the King's Council would not be allowed to remain. Most of them were sent back to their own regions through varying means of indemnities or threats offered by Richemont. Over the period of two years leading up to the Treaty of Arras, all the carousing, drunken brawls, and orgies slowed to a halt. A newfound order reigned in the royal residences.

Georges de La Tremoille was the one evil influence over the king who refused to yield to pressure and disappear. So long the chief minister to the king, La Tremoille dominated Charles as no one else could. It was La Tremoille who had had Arthur de Richemont expelled from court and La Tremoille who encouraged the king to dissociate himself from the Maid of Orléans and intimidated other good men away from the inner circle of Charles VII. He intrigued against La Hire, Xantrailles, Dunois, and even Yolande d'Aragon, and he knew better than anyone how to dissimulate events to the king. The king trusted his calculating friend to the extent that he lent a deaf ear to anyone who spoke ill of him; La Tremoille accompanied the king everywhere he went. This self-interested and evil-doing nobleman increased his own properties and fortune at the expense of the House of Valois, growing fatter and more pompous with each addition to his vast estates.

With King Charles's his rising prestige, his self-confidence improved. He gradually began to act on his own decisions and even to disagree occasionally with his favorite. La Tremoille, worried that his influence was waning as that of Richemont was on the rise, plotted the death of Richemont. Each of several attempts to end the sage Breton's life failed, and each time the would-be murderers confessed to having taken their orders from La Tremoille.

Yolande d'Aragon and Richemont decided that La Tremoille had to be removed from the court. Plotting his end began in Britanny, where most of the members of the extended royal family had met in September 1432 during the elaborate funeral of the Duchess of Britanny, who was Charles's sister Jeanne. The independent Duke of Britanny, Arthur de Richemont's brother, was prepared to renew his ties with the House of Valois, and the coming events would hasten this alliance. Together they all plotted the murder of La Tremoille.

The king himself was not present at his sister's funeral; he was in residence at the great chateau of Chinon. It was here at Chinon that he had met Joan of Arc for the first time, and here too he would meet the beautiful Agnès Sorel, his future mistress. In the spring of 1433, it was at Chinon that a band of armed men were let into the castle grounds in the middle of the night. La Tremoille was staying at Chinon, asleep in a room just across from the apartments of the king and the queen.

Led by Pierre de Brézé and Jean de Breuil, the armed men crept into the favorite's room and stabbed him in the stomach. Wounded but too fat for the stabbing to have been fatal, La Tremoille was taken to the chateau of Montrésor, the seat of Jean de Breuil. By the next morning the miscreant had agreed, in exchange for his life, to pay a ransom of 4,000 gold Ecus and to remain forever at his chateau at Sully-sur-Loire.

CHAPTER FOURTEEN

On April 16, 1443, Isabelle de Lorraine went to Saumur and René went to Angers to sign the marriage treaty of Henry VI with little Marguerite d'Anjou. This time, the King of France was not marrying France also; he was simply signing an alliance of friendship and alliance by marrying a daughter of France.

In September 1443, Charles arrived in Saumur, where he stayed until February 1444. During that period, Isabelle de Lorraine and Agnès met Charles for the first time. There is no clear record as to the date or the impact she had on the king. Isabelle de Lorraine wrote in her accounts, "January 1 to 31 July 1444—ten livres to Agnès Sorel." That was not much at the time. Agnès was probably still not a very ranking lady-in-waiting; it was later that she had become "la Dame de Beauté."

A gift of a gilded statue representing Ste. Marie Magdaleine, who became Agnès's patron saint, is in the inventory of the Collégiales at Loches in 1444. "In honor and reverence to Ste. Marie Magdaleine, the noble lady of Beauté has given this image in this church of the chateau de Loches."

The Treaty with the English dates from May 1444, as trade began with Normandy, which was at the time still under English rule.

Some say Agnès was already expecting a baby when she entered the service of the queen. Agnès was with Charles at that time, having accompanied him to Chalons and Nancy. The household of the queen was exemplary, except for little Margaret of Scotland, young wife of Dauphin Louis XI, who lived in an unreal and poetic world, sleeping little, writing poems, and apparently falling in love with poets from time to time.

So it was but in an *effacée* place that Agnès had to live as lady-in-waiting to the queen. *Décente, guindée, sévère*—the love life with the king had to be kept a great secret but not secret enough for the queen not to suffer, especially at first. Agnès's first child was a daughter, born in 1445 but died at birth.

The same year at a meeting between Burgundians and Charles, a Burgundian Olivier de la Marche said the queen, who was forty, was suffering from the painful malady called jealousy "because the king had just raised the rank of a poor young lad to such triumph and such power that her estates are comparable to those of the grandest princesses of the realm." The queen, though docile, submissive, and faithful, must have felt wounded by the recognized favorite, a royal mistress, for the first time and in her own house at her own account.

At the time, the Comte de Clermont, Pierre de Brézé, Poton de Xantrailles visited for jousts. Brézé, as Sénéchal de Poitou, became influential through friendship with Agnès. Suddenly men such as Count de Foix, Tancarville, Blainville, Bourgeois, Guillaume Jouvenel des Urssins, Jean Bureau, Etienne Chevalier, Guillaume Cousinot, and Jacques Coeur, most new men, surrounded the king. With them the king accomplished great acts: the reform of *gens de guerre,* a new basis for a standing army.

A Great Period of Romantic Poetry started in 1446. The queen gave birth to a son at Chinon on December 28, 1446, but Charles didn't bother to visit her, staying at Razilly with Agnès Sorel. However, he did send the queen 3,000 livres and a dress.

Officially called Mademoiselle de Beauté, after the name of the first seigneurerie she received from the king, Agnès was beauty itself. Olivier de la Marche wrote: "She was the most beautiful woman I have ever seen." Antoine de Chabannes, a great friend of the dauphin, said, "The most beautiful woman there ever was or ever could be." But the word Beauté was also simply a play on words, "and amongst the beauties one was held as the most beautiful in the world, and was called Mlle. De Beauté, as much for good reason as for the Chateau de Beauté near Paris, 'Montrelet.'"

Beauté was a lovely park, surrounded by walls, of which Eustache Deschamps wrote a poem for which he was famous. A square tower of three floors with pleasant light rooms where the sage Charles V could read his many books had a mill nearby, which provided a cheerful rushing water sound that enlivened the agreeable solitude.

A quittance of February 12, 1449 also gave her the seigneurerie de la Roquecezière, en Rouergue, and gave her an annual rent of 226 livres and 13 sous. She wrote in a pretty and *déliée* handwriting while signing the deed: "We, Agnès Sorel, dame de Beauté and of Roquecezière." Later she received the titles to the estates of Issoudun in Berry, and of Vernon and Anneville, in addition to her pension of 300 livres from the king. Her handwriting and manner of expression in the few letters that have survived the centuries indicated a cultivated and refined lady. It must be said that a woman of those days who could read and write with graceful penmanship were rare.

It was generally admitted that Charles must have really lost his head over Agnès. Not only did he cover her with jewels and give her important properties and the rank of a princess, which was later changed to duchess, but he could not be separated from her. Alneas Sylvius wrote, "At table, in bed, at council meetings, she is always at his side."

For the five years that Agnès lived officially as a member of the queen's household, it was evident that she had "better everything" than the queen. Chastellain, who met Agnès, had acknowledged that.

Her brothers joined the court of France shortly after she did. Charles and Jean, in 1446, were attached to the administration of the king, and two other brothers who arrived later had become simple members of the king's guards.

Agnès wasn't only young and beautiful. It was her intelligence that caused the king to change his ways. Agnès knew how to behave in every situation, and all *convenances* were respected. The first year, the king visited Agnès in the apartments of the queen, amid her ladies-in-waiting, or he received her in his apartments, supposedly in the presence of others. Both Charles and Agnès suffered from bad conscience, but Agnès truly loved the king and he was transformed by her; he had become sure of himself, outgoing, hardy, and gay.

It is said she was as generous with her *fournisseurs* (suppliers) as she was with the church and the poor.

By 1449, there appeared the first signs of luxury and ostentation in the royal family. Agnès had numerous jewels, including the first cut diamond necklace in Europe, and was one of Jacques Coeur's best clients, buying from him all sorts of riches brought back from the East: "silk carpets, rare furs, golden jewelry (American spelling as against jewellery) and colored gems." When she died Charles bought back her jewelry for 20,600 Ecus!

Unfortunately for Agnès, such ostentation had a contrary effect in a country not yet recovered from the Hundred Years Wars followed a generation later by the cruel Civil War; Agnès began to be the subject of heated criticism, from within and without the court. At a time when ladies still followed the advice of Robert de Blois and modestly covered themselves from throat to ankle, Agnès discovered that her bared shoulders and bosom were the perfect attiring exhibition to show off her newly acquired jewels. Chastellain wrote of the "hundred thousand murmurs" that rose up against Agnès because up until then she had led a life of little controversy. Apart from being the mistress of the king, she had been a conventional lady of the court in every other sense. It was scandalous to own such a rich wardrobe when the poor had only one dress meant to last forever.

Even the bishop Jouvenel advised Charles to put a stop to such flagrant expenditure for frivolity while the country was still at war, peace treaties notwithstanding. "All this pomp with trains, elaborate hairstyles, *chesnes* (old spelling for chaines) d'or, gems and other fineries displeased God and the people." He went on to say that most of the expenses were for things that didn't even come from France so the only people to profit from Agnès's excessive spending were merchants and foreigners. "You will only gain the hatred of your people…A woman is only beautiful in as much as she remains simple. Showing one's breast is only to excite one's companions, and God will punish her for this, and the king, and his people!"

The Belle Agnès's unbridled taste for luxury had to be tempered; she had thought that because of her great generosity to the poor and the church that the clergy like Jouvenel and the moralists like Chastellain would overlook her personal excesses. It was rare for Agnès to be wrong.

Olivier de la Marche, accompanying the Duchess of Burgundy to see the king, wrote once again of Agnès: "… [I]n fact, her position does much good for the kingdom of France. She has brought into the King's circle young men of arms, and good company, and ever since the king has been well-served by them." Coming from the man of the enemy Burgundy camp, this says much for Agnès's integrity and good intentions toward the king and the country.

The new men were vigorous and ready to help put the administration, the army, and the country in order. Chief of the king's men was Pierre de Brézé, long a friend of Yolande d'Aragon, who, after a glorious military career against the English, was invited to join the King's Council. From an ancient family and the minor nobility of Anjou, he proved worthy and faithful and a wise and eloquent adviser. Probably in love with Agnès but discretely so, he was, through their friendship and complicity, a powerful minister. It cannot be coincidence that the brilliant years of the reign of Charles VII corresponded precisely with the presence of his sweet mistress. It was during her six years with him that plans for the realm were carried out without delay; decisions were made rapidly and the government was at peak efficiency.

Another man in the king's new council was Jacques Coeur, and he couldn't have been more different from de Brézé. Coeur represented adventure, money, trade, and commerce. Born to a silversmith in Bourges, he travelled east to Venice, Istanbul, and Alexandria, first bringing back silver and gold, which he melted and minted in France. His motto was "à coeurs vaillants rien d'impossible" (to valiant hearts, nothing is impossible). Then he began to trade in furs, spices, silks, clothes, and jewelry. Before long he had his own mines and a huge fleet of ships and, as the richest man in France, offered to serve the king as treasurer to the crown. As such, it was he who would advance the sums to pay the debts of the royal family and the court. Another of the numerous admirers of the Dame de Beauté, he financed the king's army; without him the French could never have dreamed of chasing the English out of Normandy as quickly as they did. Trusted by Agnès, he was one of the executors of her will. Yet one account, though not credible, names him as being the one who had poisoned her to death.

The other executor of Agnès's testament was Etienne Chevalier, who, as the son of Charles's private secretary, grew up at court. Very young, sumptuous, and ostentatious, he was deeply in love with Agnès until the end of his life.

Another trusted friend was the seigneur of Villequier, a Norman who charmed the king and could make him laugh, and finally Guillaume Gouffier who had the honor, as personal valet, to sleep in the king's room.

These five loyal and intelligent men energetically and efficiently worked for the good of France while Agnès lived. It is thanks to her and to them that the king had at least a brief period of awakening that gave him the title of the Most Christian and the Very Victorious King of France for all posterity.

The dauphin, who during 1449 was the chief of Ecorcheurs, was on bad terms with René d'Anjou, was jealous of Pierre de Brézé, and probably had an adolescent passion for Agnès. It is recorded that he gave her a gift of some magnificent tapestries looted from the Armagnac château. He wanted more authority and a share in governing, had fights with his father, and once slapped Agnès. He knew that Agnès and Pierre were in his way.

More and more people began to criticize Agnès after the "gifle" of the dauphin. Agnès, in spite of impassioned pleas from the king, left court. At first she retired to the château at Loches, sometimes going to Beauté, where the king would come to stay. She never lost interest in the good of the kingdom and was always resolute when it came to the interests of the king.

Agnès died around six in the evening, on February 9, 1449, at Mesnil Farm, a dependency of Abby of Jumièges, a gem of Anglo-Norman architecture, now in ruins. She was aged 40. Although biographies were unknown at that time, chroniclers' manuscripts were circulated, such as that of Jean Chartier, the king's historian, who took great pains to hide the fact that Agnès was the king's mistress even though she had four daughters by the king who were officially recognized as daughters of the House of France. It was certainly unanimously agreed that Agnès used her great influence over the indolent Charles in a positive way that saved him his crown and his country.

In the famous painting of Agnès it seems bizarre and rather indecent that she should be bare breasted, albeit revealing only one bare breast. In later years, Diane de Poitiers and other mistresses of kings posed bare breasted for posterity. Agnès, though chaste, was the first to dare go bare.

Three of her daughters were known to have married well:

> Marie de France (1444–1473) married Olivier de Coëtivy, Sénéchal of Guyenee.

> Charlotte de Valois (ca. 1446–1477) married Jacques de Brézé, Sénéchal of Normandy, whose son Louis de Brézé would marry Diane de Poitiers (not Diane de Poitier, mistress of Henry II, who also posed bare breasted in the mid-sixteenth century), who was killed by her husband by the sword when found in the arms of a squire.

> Jeanne de Valois (1448–after 1467) married Antoine de Bueil, Chancellor of the King.

The poet Baif,[3] who paid a visit to the farm of La Ferté Mesnil, the scene of Agnès Sorel's death, wrote this ballad on the Dame de Beauté:

> *Mais la! Elle ne put rompre la destinée*
>
> *Qui pour trancher ses jours l'avait ici menée*
>
> *Où la mort la surprit. O mort! cette beauté*
>
> *Devait par sa douceur fléchir ta cruauté;*
>
> *Mais la lui ravissant à la fleur de son age*
>
> *Si grand que tu cuidais n'a esté ton outrage,*
>
> *Car si elle eût fourni l'entier nombre de jours*
>
> *Que lui pouvait donner de nature le cours,*
>
> *Ses beaux traits, son beau teint et sa belle charnure*
>
> *De la tarde vieillesse allait subir l'injure*
>
> *Et le surno de belle avecque sa beauté*
>
> *Lui fust pour tout jamais par les homes ostés;*
>
> *Mais jusques à sa mort l'ayant vue toujours belle,*
>
> *Ne pouvait lui oster le surnom de belle.*

---

[3] Jean Antoine de Baïf, the friend of Ronsard, published many poems. The first edition of his works is dated Paris 1572 and 1573.

CHAPTER FIFTEEN

The successes of Charles VII are owed principally to the riches and power of the family of his wife, Marie d'Anjou, and his mother-in-law, Yolande d'Aragon, who guided him throughout his life with her outstanding intelligence, dedication, and determination to see him crowned king of France. The other two women who played an outstanding role are Joan of Arc and Agnès Sorel. In spite of the great affection Charles had for his wife (they had by one count twenty-two children and by another count fourteen), his greatest passion was undoubtedly for his mistress Agnès Sorel. Their pillow talks are said to have influenced several major decisions affecting the kingdom. She had an assertive personality that shook the king to the foundations of his beliefs. She also played a vital part in the increasingly splendid life at the Valois Court. Her primary role in Charles's life was to encourage him and to assure him of his ability to rule, although he seemed determinedly apathetic. She managed through her determination to modify the king's old trait of mild feebleness in character.

During this period, the power of the pope was greatly diminished by the great Schism of the Occident. Thus Charles VII imposed himself as the natural chief of the Church of France. In 1438, the Pragmatic Sanction of Bourges limited the papal prerogatives and affirmed the superiority of the Councils of Bâsles and Constance over those of the Pope. This act gave the king the upper hand in nominating bishops and abbeys in monasteries and imposed important restrictions on taxes normally received by Rome on the kingdom's clergy.

Charles limited the feudal authorities and the "seigneurial" justices while creating local parliaments (Cours de Justice). He reorganized the Paris Parliament in 1454, created one in Toulouse in 1443, confirmed the one in Grenoble in 1455, and reformed the University of Paris via Cardinal d'Estrouville. Throughout his reign, Charles re-affirmed the power of the monarchy. He established a solid currency, raised the regular taxes ("la Taille since 1439"), and organized a real and permanent army with the great ordnances of 1445 and 1448. He thus reunited the kingdom around the king. He also established the University of Poitiers in 1432. His politics brought a certain prosperity to the kingdom.

The ambition of King Charles's son, the future King Louis XI, troubled the last years of his reign . His son participated in the Pragueries around 1440. The revolt in question was led by the Dauphin Louis, Duke Charles 1st of Bourbon, the Duke d'Alençon Jean II, the Duke of Britanny René d'Anjou, and other seigneurs, irritated to see their political influence and the royal favors reduced at the hands of "smaller people" surrounding the king. A first Praguerie was quickly quelled in 1437; a second (1440–1442) was much more serious; the dauphin had joined the revolt with aim to name him regent. The king occupied the Bourdonnais, the Poitou, and Auvergne, and he submitted the revolt in 1442. La Trémoille and the bastard Bourbon were thrown in the river Aube. In 1451 Jacques Coeur was arrested no doubt by jealous debtors for his personal success. He was banished in 1453.

Charles VII, as a politically intelligent and well-informed king, decided to codify all customs in the kingdom, especially those disorganizing the legal system. By the ordnance of Montils-lès-Tours in 1454, he ordered the publication of official customs, under his own authority, transforming him into "King, Fountain of Justice." According to some chroniclers, Charles VII had an abscess or gumboil in the mouth and feared being poisoned; he thus starved himself to death. He died on July 22, 1461. His son succeeded him as Louis XI.

Buried at the Saint-Denis Basilica, only King Charles's bust is still available today, after the profanation of the tombs during the Revolution in 1793.

GENEALOGY

Charles VII and Marie d'Anjou's children:

LOUIS OF FRANCE (1423–1483) who succeeds Charles as Louis XI

RADEGONDE OF FRANCE (1425–1444)

JEAN DE FRANCE (stillborn 1426)

CATHERINE OF FRANCE (1428–1446) who married in 1440 Charles le Téméraire

JACQUES DE FRANCE (1432–1437)

YOLANDE DE FRANCE (1434–1478) who married the future Duke Amédée IX of Savoie in 1452 and became Regent of Savoie upon his death

JEANNE DE FRANCE (1435–1482) who married the future Duke Jean II of Bourbon in 1452

PHILIPPE DE FRANCE (1436–1436)

MARGUERITE DE FRANCE (1437–1438)

JEANNE DE FRANCE (1438–1446)

MARIE DE FRANCE (1438–1439) twin sister of Jeanne de France

MARIE DE FRANCE (1441–died young)

MADELEINE DE FRANCE (1443–1495) who married Gaston de Foix, prince of Viane in 1462

BIBLIOGRAPHY

(PRINCIPAL RESEARCH AT THE BIBLIOTHÈQUE NATIONALE, PARIS, FRANCE)

La Vie Quotidienne de Maspero (14e, 15e, 16e siècles)

Histoire de France—LI—Charles VII Chapitre 3

Extracts of Chartrier, Berry by Denis Godefroy—Paris Imprimerie Royale 1661 in folio

Mémoires de Florent, Sire d'Illiers Capt. Au Service de Charles VII

Par Denys de Godefroy—Collection Roucher

Histoire de Charles VII par Baudot de Jully—Paris (G. de Luyne)

1er Chap. Section VII—3e n* 18

Essai Critique sur l'Histoire de Charles VII, Agnès Sorel & Jeanne d'Arc avec portraits par J. Delort—Paris Terrajeune 1824 in 8e

Histoire de Charles V le Victorieux par Pigault Lebrun—Paris Barba 1827 in 12

Journal d'un Bourgeois de Paris sous le règne de Charles VII—Collections Buchon, Michaut et Poujoulat—1st Chapt. Section VIII—3 n* 11 et 22

Le Quadrilogue Invectif d'Alain Chatrier par Brière Valigny—Reims—Impr. De P. Regnier 1850 in 8 pieces

Au Temps de Louis XIV—François Bluche—Hachette 1984

L'Enigme Charles VII par Régine Pernoud—Pourquoi il a abandonné Jeanne d'Arc—HISTORAMA N* 92—1991

Chroniques de Charles VII—Jean Chatrier et Alain Chatrier

Charles VII, roi de France et ses conseillers (1859) Auguste Vallet de Viriville

Etude sur le gouvernement de Charles VII. Thèse présentée par Hippolyte Dansin à la Faculté des lettres de Paris , Impr. De Silbermann, Strasbourg 1856

Charles VII le "roi des merveilles" par Philippe Bully—Tallandier 1994

Charles VII et son mystère par Philippe Erlanger, Gallimard, Paris 1945, Perrin 2001

Charles VII: un roi Shakespearien par Georges Minois, Perrin, Paris 2005

Jean Fouquet: An der Schewelle zur Renaissance by Claude Schaefer

A King's Mistress, or Charles VII and Agnès Sorel, and Chivalry in the fifteenth century by M. Caperfigue

La Pucelle d'Orléans, Voltaire 1762

La Pucelle d'Orléans, Schiller

Régine Pernoud, Archiviste Paléographe, Directrice du Centre de Jeanne d'Arc à Orléans:

- Vie et Mort de Jeanne d'Arc
- Pour en Finir avec le Moyen-Age (1976)
- La Femme au temps des cathédrales (1980)

Histoire de Jeanne d'Arc, Abbé Lenglet-Dufresnoy 1754 (Mémoire de la Société Archéologique et Historique de l'Orléanais)

IMAGES

Lenepveu, Jeanne d'arc au Siège d'Orléans—Jules Eugène Lenepveu historic painter depicting Joan of Arc at the Siege of Orléans

Traité de Troyes—A map of France showing various regions controlled by different factions at the time of the Treaty of Troyes; as well as Joan of Arc's journeys; the English raid in 1415; Joan of Arc and Charles VII's journey to the King's crowning in Reims

Agnès Sorel, Dame de Beauté—A portrait part of a collection of paintings owned by the Duke of Mouchy

Charles VII & Jeanne d'Arc—Comment la Pucelle (i.e. the virgin Joan of Arc) managed to influence Charles VII to give her an army!

Charles VII portrait by Fouquet, the greatest painter in France in the 15th Century

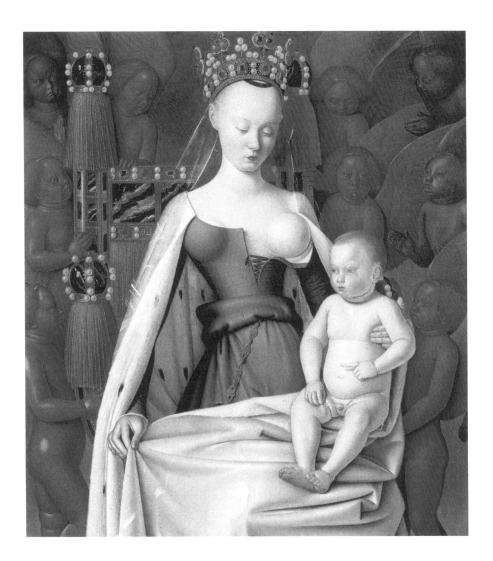

Agnès Sorel depicted in a painting as a Saint with child

Marie d'Anjou—Daughter of Louis II, Duke of Anjou and his wife Yolande; wife of Charles VII (wed in 1413, when she was 9 years old and Charles only 10.) She became Queen of France in 1422)

Miniature of Joan of Arc in full Coat of Armor

Miniature of an outdoor scene of members of the court at the entrance to a castle

Yolande d'Aragon— An astute woman, spouse of Louis II, Duke of Anjou, with good judgment and advice to Charles, well before he became King Charles VII, and still played a big role beyond the death of the Duke, in educating the future King, as well as advising the throne against the English. She and her husband Louis lived principally in Angers, in the Loire Valley